The BRICS and the Transformation of Global Power

Francesco Petrone

The BRICS and the Transformation of Global Power

Economic Expansion, Political Coordination, and Diplomatic Strategies in a Changing World Order

palgrave
macmillan

Francesco Petrone
Open University of Catalonia
Barcelona, Spain

ISBN 978-3-032-23539-8 ISBN 978-3-032-23540-4 (eBook)
https://doi.org/10.1007/978-3-032-23540-4

This Palgrave Macmillan imprint is published by the registered company Springer Nature Switzerland AG.
The registered company address is: Gewerbestrasse 11, 6330 Cham, Switzerland

Navigating Turbulent Tides: Reading the BRICS Beyond Single Stories and Old Mirrors

We are living in a time of turbulent tides—a moment of aggravated uncertainty, where storms of geopolitical rivalry, ecological collapse, technological disruption, and social fragmentation overlap in cascading ways. In this historical juncture, crises are not isolated events but increasingly intertwined, simultaneous, and mutually reinforcing. They do not simply challenge the structures of the liberal international order; they expose that many of its foundational promises—of universal governance, balanced development, and shared security—were never truly universal, having historically benefited only a limited group of states and societies, and are now visibly eroding even within their original centers.

In such a context, no single formula or hegemonic lens can offer a comprehensive interpretation of the ongoing transformation. We are in a moment where, as Antonio Gramsci famously wrote, "…the old is dying, and the new cannot yet be born; in the interregnum, a great variety of morbid symptoms appear." This book is situated precisely in this interregnum: between a fading, but still resilient liberal order and a still-forming, uncertain, plural, and experimental global architecture.

It is in this space of conceptual and institutional instability that Francesco Petrone offers us something valuable: not a prophecy, but a guide. A guide that neither romanticizes the BRICS as a revolutionary alternative to the crisis of global governance, nor demonizes them as an anti-Western anomaly. Instead, this work presents a thoughtful and intellectually rigorous examination of the BRICS as both a symptom and an active agent of global transformation—a laboratory of possibilities, shaped by contradictions, aspirations, and innovations.

Rather than approaching the BRICS through the familiar—and often limiting—filters of Western conventional categories, the author invites us to adopt new lenses that can capture their complexity and ambiguity. This means neither reducing the BRICS to a mere acronym of emerging economies, nor elevating them to the status of a counter-hegemonic project. It means recognizing the plurality they embody: a constellation of distinct trajectories and visions that materialize in their approaches to global governance and international institutions; in their reimagining of the world order through multipolarity; in their articulation of the Global South and South–South cooperation; in their propositions for sustainable development amid ecological urgency; and in their reflections on technological transformation and security.

In such a context, the vocabulary of certainty fades. The very idea of a predictable global trajectory appears fragile, as categories, institutions, and hegemonic visions that long claimed universality reveal themselves to have been limited from the outset—insufficient to interpret transformation, and even less equipped to govern it. The liberal international order, once presented as the institutional backbone of global cooperation, now exposes its inherent paradoxes: aspirational universal, yet historically selective; resilient in form, yet increasingly unable to confront planetary challenges—climate disruption, widening inequality, technological asymmetries, the inability to govern human mobility beyond securitized and exclusionary frameworks, alongside broader geopolitical realignments.

In this landscape, the BRICS have increasingly become not only an object of analysis but also an analytical lens—a window into emerging patterns, institutional experiments, and conceptual innovations. They are neither an antithesis to the West nor a nostalgic return to ideological blocs. They represent, rather, an invitation to rethink the architecture of global order from a more plural, contextual, and relational perspective.

As Chimamanda Adichie reminds us, the danger of a single story is not that it is necessarily false, but that it becomes the only story—silencing other experiences, other epistemologies, other ways of imagining the world. The BRICS do not simply offer a new story; they disrupt the longstanding monopoly of a single narrative about global order, development, and legitimacy—opening space for multiple stories to coexist, negotiate, and contest meaning.

The recent enlargement of the BRICS, together with the introduction of partner countries, has intensified this invitation. When a grouping represents 56% of the world's population, about 44% of global GDP (PPP), and spans regions and cultures, it becomes more than a diplomatic coalition: it emerges as a living reminder of the profound legitimacy deficit of current global governance. For decades, the majority of humanity—once described as the "rest of the world"—has remained structurally marginalized in international decision-making, underrepresented in agenda-setting, and systematically excluded from the institutional design of the global order. The expanded BRICS thus does not merely reflect a demographic or economic shift; it confronts the international community with a political and epistemic question: How long can rules, norms, and institutions remain legitimate if they continue to neglect those they claim to govern?

At its heart, this book shows that the BRICS matter not because they replace the liberal international order, but because they intervene in its contradictions. They insist that multilateralism must be reformed, not discarded; that development must be plural, not prescriptive; and that governance must reflect reality.

In the end, this book does not offer definitive answers. Instead, it provides a compass—a guide for navigating uncertainty, plurality, and institutional experimentation. It helps us see the BRICS not through old mirrors, but through new windows. It reminds us that in times of turbulent tides, what we need are not rigid maps, but flexible instruments of navigation; not certainties, but curiosity.

That is precisely the contribution of this book. And that is why it matters.

BRICS Policy Center
PUC-Rio, Rio de janeiro
Brazil

Marta Fernández

Competing Interests The author has no competing interests to declare that are relevant to the content of this manuscript.

Contents

About the Author

Francesco Petrone is a professor of World History and History of Philosophy in Italy and a lecturer in International Relations at the Universitat Oberta de Catalunya, Spain. He holds a PhD in Global Politics from the University of Barcelona and an MA in Political Science/International Relations from the Université Libre de Bruxelles. He has been a visiting research fellow at the BRICS Policy Center (Rio de Janeiro) and the Ralph Bunche Institute for International Studies (CUNY), New York. His research focuses on international relations, global governance, and the BRICS countries, with an emphasis on non-Western approaches, comparative climate policies, and hybrid governance. He has published widely on the BRICS, climate change, Latin America, and global governance, and collaborates with international research groups, including the BRICS Laboratory of Eurispes (Rome).

CHAPTER 1

Introduction

Abstract This introductory chapter highlights how the current international order is undergoing profound transformations that demand new analytical frameworks to be properly understood. On one hand, the Liberal International Order (LIO) appears increasingly in crisis, unable to effectively respond to global challenges that require coordinated, transnational solutions. Conceived within a post-World War II logic and primarily shaped by Western powers—namely, the US and the EU, particularly its Atlanticist component—the LIO now shows signs of obsolescence when confronted with contemporary global dynamics. On the other hand, the emergence and consolidation of the BRICS group represent a crucial shift within the international system. Far from constituting a threat to the global order, the BRICS—and now the BRICS Plus format—should be understood as a collective effort to reform traditional decision-making structures and to propose alternative visions capable of supporting a global system in transition toward multipolarity. To fully grasp what the BRICS seek to achieve, and why their role is increasingly significant, it is essential to recognize the limitations of traditional epistemological categories rooted in Eurocentric schools of thought. Instead, International Studies should broaden its analytical horizons by incorporating non-mainstream and non-Western perspectives. Such an epistemic expansion would allow for a more comprehensive and plural understanding of global transformations, particularly in this historical moment when new actors from the

F. Petrone, *The BRICS and the Transformation of Global Power*,
https://doi.org/10.1007/978-3-032-23540-4_1

Global South are asserting their voices and demanding greater participation in addressing global issues.

Keywords BRICS • Liberal International Order • Transition • Multipolarity • EU • US • Non-Western Theories

In recent years, the international landscape has undergone profound and multifaceted transformations. These changes have been continuous and unremitting, reshaping the global order across multiple domains. Within a relatively short period, the world has witnessed the emergence of a markedly altered configuration of international relations, characterized by a system in constant evolution. At present, the future trajectory of humanity—particularly regarding the organization of the global system—remains uncertain. The configuration that the international order will assume following this turbulent and, in many respects, chaotic phase is still indeterminate. At the time of writing, several armed conflicts continue to unfold across different regions of the world, underscoring the persistent incapacity of the international community to establish durable and stable ceasefires. Moreover, humanity faces a series of critical challenges that weigh heavily on global stability. Beyond the existential threat of climate change, these include recurrent migration crises, cyclical economic downturns such as the 2008 financial crisis and its enduring repercussions, the ongoing proliferation of nuclear weapons and the related security concerns, as well as the rapid and transformative rise of new technologies, which are profoundly reshaping the geopolitical order and the dynamics of interstate relations, among others.

It is often asserted that global challenges require global responses; however, what appears increasingly fragile and uncertain today is precisely the global consensus necessary to confront these challenges effectively. Paradoxically, in recent years we have witnessed a simultaneous intensification of the problems afflicting the international system and an erosion of the collective will and cooperative frameworks required to address them. Or, to cite a famous expression, we are stuck in a *gridlock* (Hale et al., 2013), which precisely prevents concrete action in the face of these challenges. Naturally, the various dimensions of these complex issues warrant systematic and comprehensive analysis. Nevertheless, this text concentrates primarily on a recent phenomenon that, in many respects, epitomizes the broader transformations currently reshaping the international system: the emergence and progressive expansion of the BRICS bloc—comprising Brazil, Russia, India, China, and South Africa.

The central arguments of this book are essentially twofold. First, it contends that the BRICS did not originate with the primary objective of contesting Western hegemony, nor can they be regarded as the principal cause of the current global disorder. Rather, the BRICS are simply a natural consequence of an international system—identified with the term *Liberal International Order* (LIO)—that is in a phase of decline, or at least experiencing a deep crisis, because it is no longer capable of solving the aforementioned problems that affect the entire planet, not just part of it. In our view, the LIO—or, more precisely, the Western-led variant of it—has long harbored inherent contradictions that have ultimately precipitated its current crisis. These internal tensions are now propelling the system not necessarily toward its dissolution, but undoubtedly toward a profound and far-reaching transformation. Certainly, several contingent factors have accelerated the decline of the LIO. Among the most significant are the 2008–2009 financial crisis, the recent COVID-19 pandemic, and the rise of populist and sovereigntist movements—particularly in Western countries, and most notably in the US—which often question or openly criticize the functioning (or malfunctioning) of the liberal system itself. More broadly, the postwar liberal order is currently facing a convergence of multidimensional shocks—health, economic, geopolitical, and ecological—that undermine both the legitimacy and the effectiveness of existing global governance mechanisms. These shocks can be described as follows: 1) Multiple and simultaneous: they span economic instability, geopolitical fragmentation, and ecological unsustainability; 2) Normatively disruptive: they erode the foundational consensus around key principles of the LIO, such as multilateralism, free trade, and liberal democracy, which are increasingly contested both externally by rising powers and internally within Western societies; 3) Institutionally revealing: they expose significant gaps and inadequacies in existing multilateral institutions, e.g., the United Nations (UN), the International Monetary Fund (IMF), and the World Trade Organization (WTO), which display a limited capacity to respond effectively to emerging global challenges.

In sum, the very structure of the LIO appears to be undergoing a profound qualitative transformation in the nature of global order itself.

The second idea underlying this book is that to understand the BRICS, we cannot use categories of international relations impregnated with Western or Eurocentric visions. Instead, we must concretely analyze the perspective these emerging (or already emerged) powers have regarding the different key points of the current international order.

In general, our impression is that these countries are often seen as a threat, a challenge, or a danger to the current world order. On the contrary, we believe that their demands precisely highlight the gaps that the LIO has been unable to fill, and thus offer alternative visions to the current international system. Of course, limitations also exist within the BRICS themselves, such as the divergent interests among member countries, the undisputed (at least for now) leadership of China, and a desire to expand their hegemony, just to name a few (we will certainly address these limitations in greater depth throughout the book). In this sense, some authors argue that the BRICS form a heterogeneous group which, due to its composite nature and internal contradictions, is destined to decline progressively over a relatively short period of time (Dubow, 2023). In our view, the BRICS group is instead destined to endure for a long time and to bring about profound changes in the international system. This is both because, as we have noted, the multiple crises characterizing it require collective global action, and because the narratives promoted by these countries are diverse—and in several cases innovative—thus offering new perspectives in various fields such as politics, economics, cooperation, and global governance. For these reasons, therefore, they really matter.

Thus, this book does not intend to be an apology for the BRICS. Instead, it seeks to show that visions complementary to the so-called single thought—the result of a dogmatism that, in Fukuyama's *end of history* (1992), saw the achievement of a perfect international system—are necessary to face today's challenges more fully, with different visions and practices, and even with alternative solutions to those that have so far proven insufficient.

The book, thus, examines some key concepts through which it outlines the BRICS' vision and compares it with the somewhat stagnant Western perspective. We believe that there is indeed a common thread linking the various topics selected. Although at first this approach might appear misleading, in reality, as we will see, the chosen themes provide valuable insight into how the BRICS' approach differs from—or at least offers an alternative to—the traditional views held by Western countries on the same issues. Thus, after an initial discussion of the formation and growth of the BRICS, and their recent plan to expand to new members (the so-called BRICS Plus), we will turn to the vision these countries hold regarding specific topics such as:

- Global governance and international institutions;
- New world order and multipolarity;
- The Global South and South–South cooperation;
- Climate change and sustainable development;
- New technologies and security.

We have carefully selected these topics—though others could certainly be added—because it is precisely in these areas that the BRICS are reshaping the global landscape. What unites the chosen themes is that each of them highlights a distinct perspective advanced by the BRICS. In essence, these countries claim that such fields should be more closely aligned with today's realities, challenging the traditional outlook that has long dominated global governance, international institutions, multilateralism, and the role of the Global South, among others. At the core of the BRICS' stance is the belief that both the theoretical frameworks and the institutional structures of the current world order fail to reflect its actual condition, namely, that it is a multipolar world. As we will see, these key subjects, which define the areas where the BRICS' voices are most forcefully expressed, are deeply interconnected. For example, reforming global governance also implies reforming international institutions, within which the BRICS demand a greater role for the Global South; multipolarity also implies broadening the perspectives through which global issues like climate change are interpreted and addressed; the diffusion and use of new technologies undoubtedly also imply a new world order and new forms of cooperation, etc. Thus, even though we address the mentioned topics separately—trying to offer a precise vision the BRICS have on each of them, a vision that inevitably contrasts with what has so far been considered mainstream—the reader will notice that links and references between these different areas will be constant.

From a methodological perspective, the analysis of these topics relies primarily on qualitative data, namely the major publications on the BRICS, journal articles, as well as writings by high-ranking policymakers, official statements, government documents, and interviews with experts on the subject. We apply this body of primary and secondary sources through a critical and comparative approach, the latter essentially focused on examining the dichotomy between the West and the Rest, of which the BRICS appear to be the main embodiment.

Faced with striking novelties such as the birth and evolution of the BRICS, interpretations tend to vary widely, often failing to grasp the full complexity of the phenomenon. It is therefore essential to specify why the BRICS are indeed an important development, with the potential to mark a clear before and after in international relations, even though other forums already exist that also attempt to address global challenges. In this text, for instance, we will discuss the G7 and the G20, but it is equally important to explain why the BRICS differ from other organizations such as the Shanghai Cooperation Organization (SCO) or even the G20 itself. In relation to the G7, the BRICS appear as an alternative force—an aspect we will analyze in greater detail in the dedicated chapter. Compared to other organizations, namely the SCO and the G20, the BRICS share with them a concern for fostering multilateral dialogue and offering alternatives to Western-centric governance structures. However, they differ significantly in scope and institutional design. The G20 is primarily an economic forum with global membership, designed to stabilize the world economy and coordinate macroeconomic policies. The SCO, by contrast, is a regional security organization with a strong geopolitical focus on Central Asia and an emphasis on maintaining peace, security, and stability, while also expanding into economic and cultural cooperation (Shanghai Cooperation Organization, 2025). The BRICS occupy an intermediate position: like the G20, they address economic and development issues, but unlike the G20 they have a smaller, more cohesive membership that explicitly seeks to reform global governance; and like the SCO, they provide a platform for non-Western voices, but without a formal security alliance structure.

A further relevant comparison can be made with the Association of Southeast Asian Nations (ASEAN). Unlike the BRICS, ASEAN is a regional organization firmly rooted in Southeast Asia, with a clear geographic identity and institutional framework aimed at promoting regional stability, economic integration, and sociocultural cooperation. Its "ASEAN Way" emphasizes consensus-building, non-interference, and gradual integration. By contrast, BRICS is not geographically confined and operates more as a coalition of emerging powers that, while diverse, share the ambition of reshaping the global order. ASEAN's strength lies in institutionalization and regional cohesion, whereas BRICS' strength lies in its symbolic and political weight as a grouping of major emerging economies with global ambitions (Porca-Konjikusic et al., 2024). Thus, both provide alternatives to Western-led governance, but while ASEAN prioritizes regional order and incremental integration, BRICS aims to create systemic impact on global governance reform. Indeed, the BRICS Plus strategy should be read in this light: in recent years, as we will see in the dedicated section, this has been driving the group toward gradual enlargement, bringing in countries that—although originating from different geographical areas of the world—share the same vision of reforming the international system.

Since the group's official formation—and as its presence consolidated and became institutionalized, reaching the current stage of attracting new member states—between 2024 and 2025 the BRICS, through the BRICS Plus strategy, added five more countries to the group: Iran, Egypt, Ethiopia, the United Arab Emirates, and Indonesia. At the same time, Saudi Arabia, although it had not initially ratified its membership (First Post, 2024), now figures as a permanent member (BRICS, 2025; Agência Brasil, 2025). During this period, many Western scholars and authors have sought to minimize the group's impact on the international stage. In general, it was initially thought that the BRICS phenomenon would be short-lived, or that over time—and even more so now with the addition of new members—the difficulty of aligning common visions would inevitably mark the end of the group.

Currently, however, reality tells a different story: the group seems motivated to strengthen cooperation and joint projects—although, it must be said, there are evident divergences and problems within the group itself—and it has even positioned itself as an alternative, both in terms of vision and diplomacy, to the world order built after World War II.

Today, the BRICS, together with its new member states and 10 additional partner countries—Belarus, Bolivia, Cuba, Kazakhstan, Malaysia, Nigeria, Thailand, Uganda, Uzbekistan, and Vietnam—represent 56% of the world's population, encompass approximately 40% of the world's territory, and account for roughly 44% of global GDP, measured in terms of purchasing power parity (Norton, 2025). Therefore, the BRICS are far from being a passing meteor, at least for now and surely for the coming years. For this reason, we believe it is essential to try to shed light on the most important aspects of the group, focusing particularly on the main topics listed above. This consolidated and continuously growing reality is destined to influence global decision-making mechanisms, diplomacy, security, international institutions, technologies, and more generally the future world order.

Thus, this book can be considered as a compass to navigate the new scenarios that the BRICS are inaugurating. Their presence, a clear sign of a shift in the international order, also testifies to the spread of new worldviews, new types of economic relations, new social and cultural approaches, and new political models that must be reckoned with—especially considering issues that affect all of us living on this planet.

The fundamental objective of this book is, therefore, to examine and elucidate the goals and aspirations of the BRICS, with the broader aim of fostering a more comprehensive and nuanced understanding of the group's position and significance within contemporary global affairs. It is our hope that, in the years to come, new bridges of dialogue and cooperation will be built to confront the pressing challenges that endanger both humanity and the stability of the international system—challenges such as climate change, migration, sustainable development, security, and the governance of emerging technologies—all of which demand coordinated global action. In this spirit, the present work seeks to offer a modest contribution toward that goal. It should be read as one among many calls to prioritize understanding over conflict, and peace over war.

Furthermore, this book is not intended to be purely academic; it also has a clear divulgative purpose. That is why we chose to address a range of timely and relevant topics, with the aim of making them accessible to a broader audience—such as graduate students in International Relations, policymakers, NGOs, or readers simply interested in gaining a more balanced and informed understanding of the BRICS. As previously mentioned, we have carefully selected these topics because it is mainly in these areas that the BRICS are transforming the global landscape. For this reason, we structured the book accordingly, dedicating a chapter to each of the main areas selected, rather than narrowing the focus to just one or two aspects, as some might suggest. There are already numerous publications that explore each of these specific issues in depth, but there is still a lack of a single volume that offers a comprehensive yet concise overview of the key dimensions of the BRICS phenomenon. We believe that providing a broader perspective may be more effective in generating interest and offering clarity. In doing so, we hope to contribute not only to academic debates, but also to the wider public discourse surrounding the evolving role of the BRICS in global affairs.

Given that today's world is in continuous and sometimes sudden upheaval, it is highly likely that within a few months or years, geopolitical scenarios will be significantly transformed.However, it is certain that the vision advocated by the BRICS, and which this book aims to analyze across the mentioned areas, will give a decisive impetus to these transformations.

References

Agência Brasil. (2025, July 6). Negotiations progress on BRICS' own payment system. https://agenciabrasil.ebc.com.br/en/internacional/noticia/2025-07/negotiations-progress-brics-own-payment-system

BRICS. (2025). About the BRICS. Retrieved January, 20, 2025, from https://brics.br/en/about-the-brics

Dubow, B. (2023, September 4). BRICS — The coalition of the globally grumpy. *Center for European Policy Analysis.* https://cepa.org/article/brics-the-coalition-of-the-globally-grumpy/

First Post. (2024, October 22). Is Saudi Arabia a Brics member or not? A curious case of invitation, acceptance and a delay. https://www.firstpost.com/world/is-saudi-arabia-a-brics-member-or-not-a-curious-case-of-invitation-acceptance-and-a-delay-13828018.html

Fukuyama, F. (1992). *The end of history and the last man.* The Free Press.

Hale, T., Held, D., & Young, K. (2013). *Gridlock: why global cooperation is failing when we need it most.* Polity Press.

Norton, B. (2025, July 04). BRICS expands to 56% of world population, 44% of global GDP: Vietnam joins as partner country. *Geopolitical Economy.* https://geopoliticaleconomy.com/2025/07/04/brics-expansion-population-gdp-vietnam/

Porca-Konjikusic, S., Hudson, P. L., Jr., & Jain, H. L. (2024). Global economic integration: How do ASEAN and BRICS organizations contribute to the process? *BRICS Journal of Economics, 5*(2), 155–168. https://doi.org/10.3897/brics-econ.5.e121010

Shanghai Cooperation Organization. (2025). General information. Retrieved October 02, 2025, from https://eng.sectsco.org/20170109/192193.html

CHAPTER 2

History of the BRICS (Up to the End of 2025)

Abstract This chapter examines how the BRICS have evolved since their inception in 2001 from a simple economic label coined by Jim O'Neill into a dynamic coalition seeking to reform global governance. Initially framed as a set of high-growth emerging economies, the group transformed into a political and institutional actor through successive summits, beginning with Yekaterinburg (2009) and Sanya (2011). South Africa's accession symbolized the bloc's aspiration to represent the Global South and enhance geographic balance, while revealing enduring tensions between inclusiveness and coherence. The establishment of the New Development Bank and the Contingent Reserve Arrangement in 2014 marked a pivotal moment, institutionalizing BRICS cooperation and offering tangible alternatives to Western-dominated financial institutions. By 2025, the NDB's regional expansion and membership enlargement—encompassing countries such as Egypt, the United Arab Emirates, Iran, and Indonesia—have consolidated BRICS as a credible instrument for financing sustainable development and strengthening South–South cooperation. Beyond economics, BRICS' agenda has expanded to encompass climate change, digital finance, and de-dollarization. The 2025 Rio de Janeiro Summit advanced the BRICS Cross Border Payment Initiative, signaling a move toward financial autonomy and multipolarity. At the same time, geopolitical frictions—especially between China and India—and external pressures, notably from the US, challenge internal cohesion.

F. Petrone, *The BRICS and the Transformation of Global Power*,
https://doi.org/10.1007/978-3-032-23540-4_2

Yet, despite such constraints, BRICS increasingly functions as both a symbolic and practical counterpoint to Western hegemony, promoting institutional pluralism, multilateralism, and inclusive governance. Its evolution illustrates the transition from descriptive economic categorization to the consolidation of a collective actor seeking to redefine the architecture of global order in the twenty-first century.

Keywords BRICS • Global governance • New development bank • De-dollarization • Multilateralism • Global South

From the Initial Idea to Diplomatic Reality

The acronym "BRIC" was coined in 2001 by Jim O'Neill, an economist at Goldman Sachs, to identify four emerging economies: Brazil, Russia, India, and China. O'Neill predicted that these countries would experience significant economic growth, increasing their share of the world's gross domestic product over the following decade. It is important to point out that his analysis was based mainly on economic indicators, without considering political aspects. The goal was to inform investors about the economies with greater growth potential compared to advanced economies. However, in just a few years, the group evolved from being merely an analytical category into building a true platform for international cooperation (Rodriguez et al., 2024).

What at first seemed like a simple acronym, created purely for descriptive purposes and to indicate promising future markets, actually triggered a whole series of initiatives that have led the BRICS to their current status, along with an expansion project already underway called BRICS Plus.

In fact, as early as July 2006, the leaders of the BRIC countries met for the first time in St Petersburg, Russia, on the sidelines of the then G8 summit. Later, in September of the same year, the BRIC foreign ministers met informally during the United Nations General Assembly. These meetings laid the groundwork for a more structured cooperation. In 2008, Russia organized a meeting with the foreign ministers of Brazil, India, and China, emphasizing the importance of dialogue based on trust, mutual respect, and common interests. This meeting marked the transition of BRIC from a simple acronym to a political and diplomatic entity (Rodriguez et al., 2024).

The evolution of the BRICS through various annual meetings has been characterized by the continuous expansion of programmatic discussion agendas and growing interest in the reform of global institutions. In 2009, the first official summit was held in Yekaterinburg, Russia, with the participation of heads of state Lula da Silva (Brazil), Dmitry Medvedev (Russia), Manmohan Singh (India), and Hu Jintao (China). On that occasion, the countries agreed to promote dialogue and cooperation in an incremental, proactive, pragmatic, open, and transparent way, aiming to build a harmonious world of lasting peace and common prosperity (BRIC, 2009). At the same time, this first meeting marked an important step toward the group's desire to consolidate its identity. From this first meeting, the image that emerged was that of a group organizing to promote cooperation among emerging countries. However, the subsequent meetings revealed a desire for a radical change in the existing international order. Thus, the BRICS became not only a group of emerging countries seeking to progressively increase cooperation but also (and above all) a real bloc presenting itself on the international stage with the aim of transforming it.

In September 2010, during a meeting on the sidelines of the United Nations General Assembly, the decision was made to invite South Africa to join the group. Its admission marked a decisive turning point in the evolution from BRIC to BRICS, formally changing the acronym into the one we know today (BRICS Expert Council, n.d.). But why was South Africa, despite being economically and demographically much smaller than the other members, included in the group? The first reason lies in the geographic balance it brought: with South Africa, the group could finally claim representation from every continent, integrating Africa, which had previously been absent (Alden & Sidiropoulos, 2011). Beyond symbolism, however, South Africa's entry reflected clear strategic calculations. For China, the country offered a gateway to Africa, a continent where Beijing was rapidly expanding its economic and diplomatic footprint (Cooper, 2011). For Brazil, it reinforced South–South solidarity and deepened ties with an African partner across the South Atlantic, advancing a shared vision of cooperation at a time when South–South trade was expected to account for a growing share of global exchanges (Besada et al., 2013). For India, South Africa's presence helped counter perceptions of the BRICS as an Asia-centric initiative dominated by China and Russia. For South Africa itself, membership elevated its international profile, giving it a voice greater than the size of its economy would otherwise warrant. It also enhanced its leadership credentials within Africa, while opening new avenues for trade and investment, both for the country and for the wider continent (Arkhangelskaya, 2013). At the same time, South

Africa's inclusion revealed some of the inherent tensions in the group's expansion. While it added legitimacy and diversity—by bringing in an African representative and signaling the BRICS' ambition to move beyond a loosely consolidated economic coalition toward a platform of global representativeness—critics pointed to its limited economic weight compared to the other members. This dilemma—how to balance inclusiveness and representativeness with cohesion and effectiveness—has resurfaced in debates over the BRICS Plus strategy. However, despite the challenges it creates for coordination and common policymaking, we believe that the BRICS Plus initiative—though undoubtedly driven by national and collective interests—also reflects the group's determination to amplify the voices of countries historically marginalized in international affairs, such as Iran.

Moreover, regarding South Africa's inclusion, although the country has acted as a bridge in opening the African continent to investment, infrastructure projects, diplomatic engagement, trade, and more, critics argue that this role is complicated by the divergent strategies of the BRICS members (Alden & Sidiropoulos, 2011). China, for instance, tends to focus on infrastructure and extractive industries; India emphasizes trade and services; Brazil prioritizes agriculture or political alignment; and Russia pursues energy and security interests. According to Bond, these differing priorities do not always align with Africa's developmental needs, effectively condemning the continent to remain underdeveloped (Bond, 2018).

In any case, South Africa officially joined by participating in the third BRICS summit, held in Sanya, China, in 2011—transforming BRIC into BRICS. Since then, the group has held annual summits, establishing itself as a political-diplomatic mechanism alternative to the traditional postwar institutions, namely, the Bretton Woods institutions (the International Monetary Fund, the World Bank, and the World Trade Organization, formerly GATT, the General Agreement on Tariffs and Trade), and as a group made up exclusively of developing countries. During the 2011 summit in Sanya, the BRICS began to openly discuss the reform of global institutions, with special attention to the international financial system, the reform of the United Nations Security Council, and the inclusion of new emerging economies in these decision-making spaces (BRICS, 2011). In 2012, a new strategic goal emerged when the BRICS began focusing more on concrete economic cooperation, introducing joint projects and signing agreements to promote trade and investment among member countries (BRICS, 2012).

The 2013 summit in Durban, South Africa, marked a turning point in the group's history, with the debate about establishing a development bank of their own—the New Development Bank (NDB)—and reserve mechanisms such as the Contingent Reserve Arrangement (CRA) (BRICS, 2013).

The following year, in 2014, the BRICS officially established the NDB and the CRA, consolidating their position as global actors determined to reform the international financial system (BRICS, 2014). In this context, the BRICS have continued to expand and strengthen their institutional framework. The creation of the NDB and the CRA represents a direct response to the perceived inefficiencies of traditional international financial institutions, often seen as biased toward Western interests. Their establishment marked a transitional phase, consolidating the group's commitment to building alternative mechanisms for international cooperation. Compared to other regional or political groupings such as ASEAN or the Non-Aligned Movement (NAM), which never developed financial institutions of global scope, the NDB signaled concrete institutionalization through tangible outputs rather than diffuse political declarations. The NDB has reinforced the BRICS by creating a coherent bureaucracy, establishing a shared organizational structure that allows members to coordinate effectively and make collective decisions while attempting to bridge political and institutional differences. At the same time, the bank has fostered social and economic embedding by integrating into member economies and supporting concrete development projects, thereby enhancing the group's legitimacy as a relevant actor on the global stage. Moreover, the NDB has begun to lay the groundwork for a normative platform capable of influencing global development finance rules and practices, even though its impact remains constrained by the political diversity of its members (Erthal Abdenur & Maiara Folly, 2015). Overall, the NDB illustrates the BRICS' ambition to reform global governance through concrete alternatives while reflecting the divergent national interests of its members. For China, the NDB complements the Belt and Road Initiative by providing multilateral legitimacy to infrastructure financing. For India and Brazil, it offers an arena to exercise influence proportionate to their size, unlike in the IMF or World Bank. For Russia, it offers a valuable financial alternative in the face of Western sanctions. For South Africa, in addition to the potential economic benefits, hosting the bank's first regional office in Johannesburg reinforces its leadership role on the African continent (Stewart et al., 2025).

Headquartered in Shanghai, the NDB has recently established several regional offices that play a crucial role in both its internal and external institutional development (Hooijmaaijers, 2021). The bank was conceived as an institution capable of providing long-term financing for infrastructure projects in developing countries, particularly across Africa, Asia, and Latin America, and was designed as an alternative to the World Bank. This bank, known as the BRICS Bank, represents a direct response to the shortcomings and limitations of traditional financial institutions, which often fail to meet the financing needs of emerging economies. Its main purpose is to provide funding for sustainable development, including infrastructure projects such as roads, railways, and renewable energy systems, aiming to accelerate economic growth in emerging markets and developing countries (EMDCs) (New Development Bank, 2025a). The NDB is also distinguished by its ability to finance projects that meet local needs and diverge from traditional policies more closely tied to the geopolitical interests of Western powers. In particular, the Bank has promoted a greater focus on sustainability and environmental protection and has proven a useful tool in addressing global challenges like climate change. By 2025, the operational role of the NDB highlights this strategy. Indeed, the BRICS are actively promoting assistance and technology transfer to the Global South. The expansion of the NDB beyond its original five members represents one of the main channels through which the BRICS consolidate their strategy. The accession of countries such as Bangladesh, the United Arab Emirates, Uruguay, Egypt, and Algeria signals not just formal enlargement but the transformation of the NDB into a multilateral institution capable of addressing shared development needs. Project-based initiatives further reinforce this legitimacy: in Bangladesh, the NDB has financed sustainable infrastructure and urban resilience projects; in Lesotho, it supported Phase II of the Lesotho Highlands Water Project, crucial for water security and climate adaptation in South Africa's Gauteng region; and Algeria, formally admitted in 2025, intends to leverage its partnership with the NDB to accelerate its energy transition, focusing on renewables, green gas, and climate adaptation in agriculture (New Development Bank, 2025b; Xinhua Institute, 2025). These examples illustrate technical cooperation and demonstrate the BRICS' ability to translate inclusive and sustainable development into practice. The growing interest from over 30 countries—including Indonesia, Mexico, Nigeria, Colombia, and Vietnam—underscores the BRICS' appeal as an alternative pole of attraction for the Global South (Stewart et al., 2025).

The NDB was established with an initial authorized capital of USD 100 billion, divided into one million shares with a par value of USD 100,000 each. The founding members subscribed to 500,000 shares, totaling USD 50 billion, of which USD 10 billion was paid-in capital and USD 40 billion callable. Subsequent accessions of new members have brought additional capital into the bank, further strengthening its financial base, with the amount expected to grow in the future as new members potentially join (New Development Bank, 2025c). The funds made available by the NDB are not tied to neoliberal economic policies, which are often embedded in the lending policies of other international institutions such as the World Bank or the International Monetary Fund (IMF). This means that the NDB has been able to develop financing policies that are more sensitive to the specific needs of developing countries without imposing economic reforms that could harm local economies.

The CRA was also created in 2014 and offers a financial safety net in case of economic crises, allowing member countries to reduce their dependence on the resources and interventions of Western institutions, which often impose strict economic and political conditions. Thus, the CRA has been established as a reserve network to help BRICS countries respond to financial crises and provide liquidity in the event of external shocks—such as currency fluctuations or international financial market crises—allowing countries in difficulty to access low-cost liquidity and avoid dependence on relief mechanisms, particularly those operated by the IMF. This latter institution, moreover, had already been criticized by several Western authors, including Stiglitz (2002), for their austerity policies and for creating major dependencies in developing countries through the creation of heavy debt.

With a fund of $100 billion, the CRA provides short-term financial assistance to the group's members in case of need, but also to other developing countries facing economic difficulties. This tool has strategic importance for the economic stability of BRICS countries, as it offers an autonomous alternative to the international financing instruments dominated by Western actors, providing greater independence in the economic policies of the group's members.

The creation of the CRA and NDB marked a break with the traditional international order, demonstrating that the BRICS countries are capable of building an economic solidarity system that challenges the global leadership of financial institutions established in the postwar period. At the same time, it represents a response to the financial vulnerabilities that many emerging countries must face in an unstable global economic system.

In any case, some clarifications are necessary. It is clear that, in terms of scale, economic capacity, and the current reach of their projects, the NDB and the CRA are not yet able to compete with much larger and economically more powerful financial institutions with a far broader scope. For instance, the NDB does not even rank among the 20 largest development banks in the world (N.D., 2024). However, what matters most—and what makes these institutions highly significant—is not their quantitative dimension but their symbolic and strategic value. Their importance lies less in the size of their current operations than in their normative and political function as instruments of institutional diversification and voice redistribution within the global financial architecture. That is to say, these institutions represent a deliberate attempt to build alternatives to Western-dominated structures, such as the IMF and the World Bank. Moreover, their governance models—particularly the principle of equal voting rights within the NDB—constitute an experiment in institutional equity, standing in contrast to the weighted voting systems that characterize the Bretton Woods institutions (as will be examined in the dedicated chapter). In this sense, their relevance lies not in their current size, but in their capacity to embody and advance a broader process of institutional pluralization and to challenge established hierarchies within global governance. Accordingly, this analysis focuses on their political symbolism and their potential transformative role in shaping the future dynamics of global governance.

The Further Evolution of a Global Governance Actor

The expansion of the BRICS was a central topic at the 2015 summit in Ufa, Russia, where the group's leaders confirmed their intention to include new members and emphasized strengthening multilateralism, economic and financial cooperation, and addressing global challenges such as terrorism (BRICS, 2015). The 2016 summit in Goa, India, saw discussions on inclusive and sustainable growth, with particular attention to reducing economic inequality among members (BRICS, 2016). In the following years, the BRICS continued to strengthen economic and political cooperation, while maintaining a focus on reforming the global financial system and promoting a more equitable and multilateral global governance. The BRICS group, therefore, sought and is indeed exercising an increasing impact on the international system that, until now, had been dominated by Western countries, primarily the US and Western Europe, throughout most of the twentieth century.

In 2017, the debate on expansion took a concrete form with discussions on admitting new members. The BRICS began seriously considering the idea of including new developing countries that shared the group's core principles, such as support for multilateralism, commitment to sustainable development, and promotion of a more inclusive global governance (BRICS, 2017).

This issue has been debated in the group's various annual meetings, with several countries—such as Indonesia, Mexico, Turkey, and Iran—expressing interest in joining the group. In the group's opinion, this expansion, which is already underway, could strengthen the voices of non-Western countries on the world stage. At the same time, this expansion could also test the internal unity of the group, which will have to deal with the different political and economic requirements of the new members.

In 2020, during the virtual summit chaired by Russia, the BRICS countries reiterated their vision of a multipolar world, emphasizing the importance of greater representation of emerging economies in global institutions, particularly the aforementioned global governance institutions, such as the IMF and the World Bank (BRICS, 2020). The issue of global governance reform and sustainability was the center of the debate, even in the context of the health and economic crisis caused by the COVID-19 pandemic, which accelerated the need for a more resilient and inclusive global system. The evolution of the BRICS, therefore, is not just a process of expanding the group, but also a path of transformation aimed at defining a new global governance architecture that can more effectively respond to the challenges of the twenty-fir century.

In the following years, the BRICS expanded their cooperation beyond economics, including sectors such as health, security, and development. This evolution led to delicate and sometimes controversial interactions among the members, influencing bilateral and multilateral relations within the group. Despite the challenges, the BRICS have played a strategic role in promoting a multipolar world order, based on the principles of justice, reducing inequality, and rethinking global governance.

In 2023, the BRICS finally began the expansion process by inviting new members such as Argentina, Iran, the United Arab Emirates, Egypt, and Ethiopia (although Argentina withdrew from the accession in 2024, after Javier Milei's election as president). This expansion, known as the BRICS Plus (or BRICS+) initiative, aims to increase the political and economic weight of the group, with a particular focus on de-dollarization. At the same time, this expansion seeks to strengthen the representation of emerging economies and promote a fairer global governance system.

In 2024, the group announced the start of the actual expansion with the inclusion of Egypt, the United Arab Emirates, Ethiopia, and Iran, followed by Indonesia in 2025, forming the first expanded core of the BRICS Plus strategy.

The Challenge to Western Supremacy: The Battle Against the Dollar and the Focus on Climate Change

The expansion of the BRICS, however, has raised concerns in several Western countries. For example, in January 2025, President Donald Trump threatened to impose a 100% tariff on the member countries of the group if they attempted to replace the US dollar as the world's reserve currency. This statement reflects the geopolitical tensions associated with the rise of the BRICS as an alternative economic power. In the end, 50% tariffs were applied to India and Brazil—likely with the aim of weakening these countries, and more broadly, to undermine the BRICS as a whole. However, this measure appears to be strengthening ties among the BRICS members, as evidenced by India's participation in the 2025 SCO summit, where the iconic image of the presidents of Russia, India, and China warmly greeting each other and shaking hands seemed to signal a closer alliance and foreshadow the intention to inaugurate a new world order (India Today, 2025).

One of the main objectives of the BRICS is, in any case, to reduce dependency on the US dollar in international trade. China and Russia have increased the use of their own currencies in bilateral transactions, while Brazil has proposed the creation of a common currency for the bloc and, at the beginning of its presidency in 2025, launched an initiative to propose the use of blockchain technology among the countries to facilitate trade and financial transactions. In July 2025, during the 17th BRICS Summit in Rio de Janeiro, the member countries advanced the creation of an alternative payment system to SWIFT, as part of the

BRICS Cross-Border Payment Initiative (BRICS, 2025), developed by the Central Bank of Brazil and the Ministry of Finance. This initiative, together with the BRICS Interbank Cooperation Mechanism, aims to make financial transactions among BRICS countries more accessible, faster, and secure, while reducing dependence on the US dollar and platforms controlled by Western powers. Brazilian President Luiz Inácio Lula da Silva has emphasized that the goal is not to replace national currencies but to promote a multipolar international financial system and strengthen economic cooperation within the bloc (Barcellos, 2025). The initiative is expected to leverage blockchain technology and the NDB as an incubator for new financial instruments and institutional support. Additional measures include the creation of regional reinsurance systems, settlement and custody infrastructures, and the strengthening of the CRA, with the broader aim of building an autonomous financial ecosystem that protects member countries from unilateral sanctions and enhances their monetary and financial autonomy. Supported for years by China and Russia, this initiative represents a concrete step toward the de-dollarization of international trade and a formal incorporation of Brazil's priorities as BRICS chair in 2025 (Chagas, 2025).

The tariff policies of the US have shaken the global economy, exerting pressure on international trade networks (BBC News, 2025). In the face of this challenge, it is highly likely that the BRICS nations and other emerging economies will seek to further strengthen regional cooperation and make greater use of multilateral mechanisms to defend their interests and counter unilateralism. In this sense, the current international situation pushes BRICS even further to assert the fundamental role of multilateralism and global cooperation, especially in a context where the US administration continues to impose tariffs on its trading partners, including BRICS countries.

Protectionist policies, particularly the "America First" strategy of the Trump administration, have compromised the multilateral trading system, destabilizing supply chains and increasing uncertainty for businesses. For developing countries, these unilateral measures have worsened economic difficulties, limiting exports and complicating integration into global markets. Many nations, to avoid tariff escalation, have been forced to make onerous concessions, often at the cost of their long-term economic development. Furthermore, attempts to redesign global supply chains could exacerbate tensions between emerging economies, fueling harmful competition and reinforcing structural inequalities.

In this scenario, the role of BRICS as representatives of growing economies becomes increasingly crucial. The IMF has predicted that, in the coming years, the world economy will increasingly rely on BRICS for growth, rather than Western countries (Tanzi, 2024). This combined economic force allows the BRICS to act as a bulwark against unilateralism and promote a fairer trade system. It is important to note that, while BRICS benefit from access to US markets, the US also depends on the products and supply chains of BRICS countries. For this reason, the imposition of high tariffs would harm not only emerging economies but also the US productive system, compromising essential trade flows. This demonstrates the need for trade policies based on cooperation rather than unilateral measures. Unilateral actions, in addition to being ineffective in addressing global challenges, risk compromising international economic stability. One only has to recall, for example, the devastating effects of autarkic and protectionist policies following the 1929 crisis in the US, which decisively influenced the escalation toward World War II.

Given this troubling situation, BRICS and other developing countries could strengthen their commitment to a more cohesive multilateralism, aiming to protect the interests of the Global South and promote a more stable and just world economy. This involves a constant defense of multilateralism principles, deeper economic cooperation, and the strengthening of trade ties. At the national level, BRICS countries should promote industrial innovation and improve competitiveness. At the regional level, it is necessary to encourage trade and investment liberalization to create a more favorable environment for economic cooperation. Another strategic area is the coordination of global supply chains. By strengthening collaboration across different productive segments, BRICS can optimize resource management and promote synergistic development. This consolidation strengthens the role of BRICS as key players in a more inclusive economic system, in which all nations have a voice, not just those with greater military or economic weight.

The emergence of BRICS as a geopolitical force, therefore, demonstrates that the world order is no longer dominated by a single power. Despite statements from Donald Trump, who referred to BRICS as "dead" due to the tariffs imposed by his administration, data shows the opposite (Powell, 2025). As previously mentioned, with the entry of Indonesia as an official member, and Malaysia as a partner country in January 2025, the BRICS countries represent more than 56% of the global population and account for 44% of the world's GDP in nominal terms (Norton, 2025).

The BRICS decision-making model, based on consensus and aligned with the principles of the United Nations, contrasts with the US' growing preference for bilateralism, which tends to divide and fragment negotiations in favor of its own "America First" agenda. In contrast, the BRICS approach proposes, at least as proclaimed in various summits and as a result of the implementation of the BRICS strategy, a stable alternative for a multipolar world, valuing the voices of emerging economies and counteracting the return to dynamics of economic domination. As the world moves further away from unipolar hegemony, the BRICS model offers a vision of governance that is more equitable, where even developing countries can potentially influence the global agenda. Resisting the pressures of bilateralism and power dynamics is essential to ensure that multipolarity translates into balanced cooperation, rather than new forms of division and exploitation. In this context, the BRICS are positioned as key players in building a more inclusive and sustainable global order (Powell, 2025).

The group is, therefore, at a moment of transition: on one hand, the expansion and strengthening of cooperation in key sectors indicate growing geopolitical ambition; on the other hand, internal divergences and external pressures (especially from the US and the EU) threaten to compromise long-term strategic cohesion. In this context, the future of the group will depend on its ability to overcome internal divisions and structure a more effective governance, turning its ambitions into concrete actions on the international stage.

Since its creation, the group has been conceived as a platform for cooperation among emerging economies to reform global institutions and improve their influence in international economic and political dynamics. The goal of this platform was to go beyond the world order dominated by Western powers, aiming to create an international system that more equitably represented the needs of developing economies. The five original countries—Brazil, Russia, India, China, and South Africa—and those that have joined later, are united by a common will to promote an international architecture that favors the multiplicity of voices and viewpoints, in contrast to the unilateral approach that has characterized decisions in global institutions such as the IMF, World Bank, and the World Trade Organization (WTO).

As mentioned, the BRICS were born as a platform for dialogue and cooperation among emerging economies that, although very different in terms of size and political and cultural histories, share the goal of reforming global institutions and reducing the power gap between the Western world and developing economies. Geopolitical tensions and global challenges, such as the 2008 economic crisis and climate change, have led the group to seek alternative solutions to the traditional models dominated by the G7 and the aforementioned international financial organizations.

In this context, the creation of new institutions such as the abovementioned NDB and CRA has marked a crucial step in the institutionalization of the BRICS. It has represented a genuine alternative turning point, even though these institutions are still relatively "young," in contrast to the traditional international institutions stemming from the Bretton Woods system—such as the IMF—which, according to the BRICS, remain dominated by an excessive and increasingly outdated Western influence, especially given the current multipolar nature of the world. A more in-depth discussion of this point will follow in the dedicated chapter. However, the growing influence of the BRICS is not limited only to the economic sphere but also extends to international politics, particularly through the promotion of a more inclusive and multipolar system of global governance. This process of reforming global institutions is fueled by a shift in political and economic priorities, where BRICS countries, and especially China, are trying to propose an alternative vision to traditional Western politics, which is often characterized by a free-market approach and the protection of Western economic interests. This vision, therefore, is fundamentally based on a break from traditional Eurocentrism and Anglocentrism, and instead seeks to promote greater inclusion of those countries that have historically had marginal, if not completely nonexistent, roles in the formulation of global policies.

At the same time, a unilateral vision of global issues, according to them, would hinder addressing global problems that affect the entire hemisphere. A specific example is climate change, one of the most urgent problems we face today, and which, with traditional approaches that also limit the voice of those most vulnerable to its effects (i.e., the countries of the Global South), represents an obstacle to a truly holistic approach to the issue. Just to give an example: China, with its growing economic and political influence, plays a key role in this process. In particular, China's proposed "ecological civilization" perfectly fits into this new paradigm. The idea of a holistic approach to environmental and natural resource management is at the core of Chinese policy, which seeks to promote an integrated vision that balances the needs of economic development with ecological sustainability. Notably, there are early signs from China that this approach may be yielding results: in the first half of 2025, CO_2 emissions reportedly fell by approximately 1% compared to the previous year (World Energy, 2025). This approach contrasts sharply with the more traditional Western capitalist model, which tends to prioritize economic growth and cost reduction, often at the expense of the environment. The extreme case of the Trump administration exemplifies this divergence: the US withdrew from the 2015 Paris Agreement, and during the 2025 UN General Assembly in New York, President Trump strongly criticized climate policies, even expressing skepticism about the very existence of climate change. Specifically, at the UN General Assembly, Trump stated that: "All of these predictions (climate change) made by the United Nations and many others, often for bad reasons, were wrong. They were made by stupid people that of course their countries' fortunes and given those same countries, no chance for success. If you don't get away from this green scam, your country is going to fail" (United Nations, 2025).

The BRICS, with their proposal for an alternative economic system and their ability to influence global policies, are trying to create a world where geopolitical dynamics are not dominated by a few actors. The intention to strengthen the role of non-Western countries in global institutions, both political and economic, is clear, and the group has used several instruments to achieve this, including the creation of the financial institutions mentioned earlier. Therefore, the BRICS group is becoming an increasingly important actor in shaping global policies, particularly in crucial areas such as climate governance, natural resource management, and the reform of international financial institutions.

In the context of climate governance, the BRICS could play a decisive role in defining the future of international climate agreements, highlighting the need for more equitable approaches that take into account the economic and political specifics of each country. Additionally, the introduction of new narratives and sustainable development models by the BRICS countries could have a profound impact on global political decisions, favoring a restructuring of global governance that reflects the challenges of the twenty-first century. The potential entry—or at least a significant rapprochement—of the EU into the BRICS group, although currently unlikely but supported by some authors (Euractiv, 2024), could accelerate this process, fostering broader dialogue among major global actors on climate change management and international institutional reform.

In any case, the current international scenario represents a significant challenge for Western powers, which might have to adapt to a new global order that includes more voices and different approaches to managing global problems. The expansion of the BRICS, which could include the entry of more new countries in the future, would contribute to reshaping the architecture of global governance, leading to a more complex and possibly more inclusive system.

Internal Dynamics and Geopolitical Challenges

Although the BRICS are presented by the group's supporters as a cohesive bloc, there are deep divergences among its members. Some of the main sources of tension include:

- **Economic and political differences**: China is by far the dominant economy in the group, with a GDP greater than the sum of the other members. This imbalance may generate mistrust among the other countries, which are concerned about possible Chinese hegemony. China's growing economic influence, along with its increasing political and military power, fuels fears of disproportionate control over the BRICS agenda. Additionally, China's ability to invest massively in infrastructure and strategic projects in developing countries gives it considerable weight in collective decisions. This concern is reflected in the efforts of other members to balance China's influence by promoting initiatives that strengthen economic and political cooperation within the group. For example, India has sought to diversify its strategic and economic alliances to counter China's growing dominance, while Brazil, Russia, and South Africa attempt to maintain a more pragmatic approach, seeking short- and medium-term economic and political benefits. Overcoming these differences will be crucial for the BRICS to consolidate their role as a cohesive and relevant bloc in global governance.
- **Geopolitical divergences**: India and China have tense relations due to territorial disputes along the Himalayan border. However, in this case, it should be noted that the 2024 Summit in Kazan, Russia, represented a moment of easing tensions between the two countries on this issue, as both powers signed agreements for joint border patrols (*Hindustan Times*, 2024; McCarthy & Iyer, 2024). Furthermore, Russia's position, isolated from the West due to the

war in Ukraine, has created a complex dynamic within the group. Indeed, while Russia has been able to count on various markets for its products, such as gas and oil, the stance of the other BRICS countries has always been in favor of dialogue and, therefore, the peaceful resolution of the conflict.

- **Effective capacity to influence the global order**: While the BRICS group has increased its cooperation in sectors such as health and security, it is still premature to speak of an effective capacity to influence global decisions and the international order, which is currently in a phase of transition. It is true that the group's growth is happening rapidly, and this expansion through BRICS Plus will present new internal challenges, precisely due to the increasing number of countries, which may affect the common vision.

Despite internal challenges and differences among members, the BRICS countries remain an important force in the global economy, contributing to reshaping the world order and promoting greater cooperation among emerging economies.

Summary of the Summits Since 2009

2009 – Ekaterinburg, Russia

- First BRIC Leaders' Summit (before South Africa's entry in 2011)
- Declaration of the group's main objectives: promotion of dialogue, cooperation, and management of the global financial crisis
- Support for reform of international financial institutions (IMF and World Bank)

2010 – Brasilia, Brazil

- BRICS leaders formalized the annual rotation of the presidency
- Definition of action plans for future cooperation

2011 – Sanya, China

- South Africa joins the BRICS countries, expanding the group to five members
- Adoption of fundamental principles: openness, pragmatism, solidarity, and neutrality with respect to third countries

2012 – New Delhi, India

- Proposal for the creation of the BRICS Development Bank (NDB) to finance infrastructure projects in emerging countries

2013 – Durban, South Africa

- Expansion of cooperation with the African Union and regional organizations
- Strengthening of trade and investment ties among BRICS countries

2014 – Fortaleza and Brasilia, Brazil

- Official establishment of the NDB
- Creation of the BRICS Contingent Reserve Arrangement (CRA) to protect their economies from global financial crises

2015 – Ufa, Russia

- Operationalization of the NDB and CRA
- Adoption of the Ufa Declaration and Action Plan
- Cultural and economic cooperation agreements

2016 – Panaji, India

- Goa Declaration: common positions on global security, economic cooperation, trade, and poverty reduction
- Creation of the BRICS Stock Exchanges Alliance

2017 – Xiamen, China

- Launch of the BRICS Plus initiative to engage other emerging economies
- Strengthening of trade and financial relations

2018 – Johannesburg, South Africa

- Focus on the Fourth Industrial Revolution and cooperation in science and technology

- Greater involvement with developing economies

2019 – Curitiba, Brazil

- Focus on WTO reform, innovation, and economic growth

2020 – Virtual Summit, Russia

- Coordination of the response to COVID-19, support for the World Health Organization, and collaboration on vaccines

2021 – Virtual Summit, India

- Adoption of the BRICS Action Plan against Terrorism

2022 – Virtual Summit, China

- Initiatives for Global Development to accelerate the Sustainable Development Goals

2023 – Johannesburg, South Africa

- Expansion of BRICS: Egypt, the United Arab Emirates, Ethiopia, and Iran set to join in 2024 (pending Saudi Arabia's ratification and Argentina's withdrawal)

2024 – Kazan, Russia

- Further BRICS expansion
- Adoption of the Kazan Declaration (134 points)
  - UN reform: support for a more democratic and representative Security Council
  - Opposition to unilateral sanctions hindering the development of emerging countries
  - Support for the creation of a sovereign Palestinian state and its entry into the UN
  - Commitment to the peaceful resolution of global conflicts (Middle East, Ukraine, etc.)
  - Condemnation of terrorist attacks

- Economic cooperation: support for WTO reform and Russia's proposal for a "Grain Exchange"
- Exploration of an independent system for BRICS cross-border payments

2025 – Rio de Janeiro, Brazil

- Expansion and inclusivity of the group: official entry of Indonesia, Iran, Egypt, Ethiopia, and the United Arab Emirates, bringing the number of members to 10
- Artificial intelligence and global governance: importance of developing AI technologies that are inclusive and respectful of human rights
- Sustainability and climate justice
- Condemnation of terrorism and commitment to peace
- Criticism of unilateral policies and tariffs

BRICS Cooperation Structure

- Regular meetings at different levels:
  - Annual summits between leaders
  - Meetings within the framework of the G20 and UN General Assembly
  - Ministerial meetings on finance, trade, foreign relations, agriculture, etc.
  - Judicial and business cooperation through research institutions and trade associations
  - Coordination in the United Nations (New York, Geneva, Vienna), UNESCO (Paris), and other international organizations

References

Alden, C., & Sidiropoulos, E. (2011, April 13). South Africa, Africa and the BRICS: The apex of the South?. *SAIIA*. https://saiia.org.za/research/south-africa-africa-and-the-brics-the-apex-of-the-south/

Arkhangelskaya, A. A. (2013). The Republic of South Africa – the new member of BRICS. In V. A. Nikonov & G. D. Toloraya (Eds.), *The strategy of Russia in BRICS: Goals and tools*. RUDN.

Barcellos, T. (2025, December 03). Sem provocar Trump, Brasil quer propor tecnologia cripto para o comércio entre países do Brics, *O'Globo*. https://oglobo.

globo.com/economia/noticia/2025/03/12/sem-provocar-trump-brasil-quer-propor-tecnologia-cripto-para-o-comercio-entre-paises-do-brics.ghtml
BBC News. (2025, April 3). Los aranceles de Trump son el mayor cambio en el comercio global en 100 años y una guerra comercial mundial parece inevitable. https://www.bbc.com/mundo/articles/c1wdj4x1j92o.
Besada, H., Tok, E., & Winters, K. (2013). South Africa in the BRICS: Opportunities, challenges and prospects. *Africa Insight, 42*(4), 1–15. https://scholar.google.com/citations?view_op=view_citation&hl=en&user=1_BwDl0AAAAJ&pagesize=100&citation_for_view=1_BwDl0AAAAJ:Y0pCki6q_DkC
Bond, P. (2018). Can the BRICS Re-open the "gateway to Africa"? South Africa's contradictory facilitation of divergent Brazilian, Russian, Indian and Chinese Interests. In D. Nagar & C. Mutasa (Eds.), *Africa and the world*. Palgrave Macmillan. https://doi.org/10.1007/978-3-319-62590-4_18
BRIC Leaders Meeting. (2009, January 16). The 1st BRIC Summit; Yekaterinburg Declaration, Russia. http://en.kremlin.ru/supplement/209.
BRICS Expert Council – Russia. (n.d.). The history of BRICS. Retrieved October 01, 2025, from https://bricscouncil.ru/en/history
BRICS Leaders Meeting. (2011, April 14). The 3rd BRICS Summit, Sanya Declaration. https://brics.br/pt-br/documentos/acervo-de-presidencias-anteriores/leaders-declarations/2011-iii-bric-summit-sanya-declaration.pdf
BRICS Leaders Meeting. (2012, March 29). The 4th BRICS Summit, Delhi Declaration. https://www.mea.gov.in/bilateral-documents.htm?dtl/19158/.
BRICS Leaders Meeting. (2013, March 27). The 5th BRICS Summit, eThekwini/Durban Declaration: "BRICS and Africa – Partnership for Development, Integration and Industrialisation." https://brics.br/en/documents/collection-of-previous-presidencies/leaders-declarations
BRICS Leaders Meeting. (2014, July 15). The 6th BRICS Summit: Fortaleza Declaration, Brazil. http://www.brics.utoronto.ca/docs/140715-leaders.html
BRICS Leaders Meeting. (2015, July 09). The 7th BRICS Summit: Ufa Declaration, Russia. http://www.brics.utoronto.ca/docs/150709-ufa-declaration_en.html
BRICS Leaders Meeting. (2016, October 16). The 8th BRICS Summit: Goa Declaration, India. http://www.brics.utoronto.ca/docs/161016-goa.html
BRICS Leaders Meeting. (2017, September 04). The 9th BRICS Summit: Xiamen Declaration, China. http://www.brics.utoronto.ca/docs/170904-xiamen.html.
BRICS Leaders Meeting. (2020, November 17). The 12th BRICS Summit: Moscow Declaration, "BRICS Partnership for Global Stability, Shared Security and Innovative Growth." http://www.brics.utoronto.ca/docs/201117-moscow-declaration.html
BRICS Leaders Meeting. (2025, July 06). The 17th BRICS Summit: Rio de Janeiro Declaration, Brazil. https://brics.br/en/documents/presidency-documents/250705-brics-leaders-declaration-en.pdf/

Chagas, R. (2025, July 7). De-dollarization: BRICS leaders propose creating an alternative payment system to SWIFT. *Brasil de Fato*. https://www.brasildefato.com.br/2025/07/07/de-dollarization-brics-leaders-propose-creating-an-alternative-payment-system-to-swift

Cooper, A. F. (2011, April 13). The diplomatic logic of South Africa's entry into BRICS. *World Politics Review*. https://www.worldpoliticsreview.com/the-diplomatic-logic-of-south-africas-entry-into-brics/.

Erthal Abdenur, A., & Folly, M. (2015). The new development bank and the institutionalization of the BRICS. *R/evolutions: Global Trends & Regional Issues, 3*(1), 66–92.

Euractiv. (2024, October 24). The Brief – What if the EU were part of the BRICS?. https://www.euractiv.com/opinion/the-brief-what-if-the-eu-would-part-of-brics/

Hindustan Times. (2024, December 3). India-China relations have progressed: S Jaishankar in Lok Sabha. https://www.hindustantimes.com/india-news/indiachina-relations-have-progressed-s-jaishankar-in-lok-sabha-101733216118721.html

Hooijmaaijers, B. (2021). The internal and external institutionalization of the BRICS countries: The case of the New Development Bank. *International Political Science Review, 43*(4), 481–494. https://doi.org/10.1177/01925121211024159

India Today. (2025, September 02). Is Trump chaos giving birth to a new world order?. https://www.indiatoday.in/india/story/pm-modi-sco-summit-china-president-xi-russia-vladimir-putin-multipolarism-trump-tariff-unipolar-stance-explained-2779993-2025-09-02

McCarthy, S. & Iyer, A. S. (2024, October 23). India and China have struck a deal that could ease border tensions ahead of expected leader meeting. *CNN*. https://edition.cnn.com/2024/10/22/asia/india-china-border-agreement-intl-hnk/index.html.

N.D. (2024, February 12). The 20 largest global development banks and their relevance for geopolitics. *The Atlas Report*. https://atlas-report.com/the-20-largest-global-development-banks-and-their-relevance-for-geopolitics/

New Development Bank. (2025a). About NDB. Retrieved September 24, 2025, from https://www.ndb.int/about-ndb/

New Development Bank. (2025b). All projects. Retrieved August 28, 2025, from https://www.ndb.int/projects/all-projects/

New Development Bank. (2025c). Shareholding. Retrieved September 23, 2025, from https://www.ndb.int/about-ndb/shareholding/

Norton, B. (2025, July 04). BRICS expands to 56% of world population, 44% of global GDP: Vietnam joins as partner country. *Geopolitical Economy*. https://geopoliticaleconomy.com/2025/07/04/brics-expansion-population-gdp-vietnam/.

Powell, W. (2025, May 03). A crucial counterbalance. *China Daily Global.* https://www.chinadaily.com.cn/a/202503/05/WS67c79e3ea310c240449d8a20.html

Rodriguez, M. E., Fernández, M., & Guimarães Canellas de Oliveira, R. (2024). Caderno para entender o BRICS (BPC Papers, V.11, N. 06, Dezembro 2024). *BRICS Policy Center.* https://bricspolicycenter.org/wpcontent/uploads/2025/02/CADERNO_BRICS_19x25-compactado.pdf

Stewart, P. et al. (2025, March 31). BRICS Expansion and the future of world order: Perspectives from member states, partners, and aspirants. *Carnegie Endowment for International Peace.* https://carnegieendowment.org/research/2025/03/brics-expansion-and-the-future-of-world-order-perspectives-from-member-states-partners-and-aspirants.

Stiglitz, J. E. (2002). *Globalization and its discontents.* Penguin.

Tanzi, A. (2024, October 23). IMF sees growth shift towards Brics and away from g7 in new outlook. *Bloomberg.* https://www.bloomberg.com/news/articles/2024-10-23/imf-sees-growth-shift-toward-brics-away-from-g7-in-new-outlook

United Nations. (2025, September 24). Trump criticizes climate policies at UN General Assembly. https://news.un.org/en/story/2025/09/1165924

World Energy. (2025, August 22). *China's carbon emissions fell in the first half of 2025, study shows.* https://www.world-energy.org/article/53504.html

Xinhua Institute. (2025, July 16). BRICS cooperation: Advancing the collective progress of the Global South. *Report realised during the BRICS Media and Think Tank Forum in Rio de Janeiro.* https://www.tralac.org/documents/resources/external-relations/brics/5998-brics-cooperation-advancing-the-collective-progress-of-the-global-south-xinhua-institute/file.html

CHAPTER 3

Global Governance and International Institutions

Abstract This chapter explores the BRICS' vision of global governance and its implications for the reform of international institutions such as the United Nations, the International Monetary Fund, and the World Bank. Emerging as a coalition of major non-Western powers, the BRICS (Brazil, Russia, India, China, and South Africa) seek to transform the postwar Liberal International Order , which they regard as outdated, exclusionary, and reflective of Western geopolitical dominance. For the BRICS, global governance must be restructured to reflect contemporary multipolar realities and ensure a more equitable distribution of voice and representation within international decision-making bodies. Their critique targets the persistence of hierarchical power relations and conditionalities imposed by Western-led institutions, which, according to the BRICS, constrain national sovereignty and perpetuate economic dependency. In response, the group has developed alternative mechanisms such as the New Development Bank and the Contingent Reserve Arrangement, aimed at fostering South–South cooperation, sustainable development, and financial autonomy. These institutions not only complement existing global frameworks but also signal a paradigm shift toward a more inclusive and plural form of multilateralism. The EU, by contrast, continues to champion a rule-based international order rooted in legal conditionality, democratic norms, and human rights. While this model has contributed to stability and institutionalization, it often clashes with the BRICS'

F. Petrone, *The BRICS and the Transformation of Global Power*,
https://doi.org/10.1007/978-3-032-23540-4_3

emphasis on sovereignty, mutual respect, and non-interference. The tension between these two approaches reflects broader debates over the nature of legitimacy, governance, and norm diffusion in a rapidly changing world. Rather than representing a zero-sum confrontation, the interaction between the EU and the BRICS may lead to a hybridization of global governance, where Western normative frameworks coexist and gradually integrate with alternative, non-Western perspectives. Such hybridization could pave the way for a more adaptive and balanced international system—one that combines the strengths of institutional discipline with the inclusiveness and pluralism required to manage global interdependence in the twenty-first century.

Keywords BRICS • Global Governance • Institutional Reform • European Union • United Nations • Hybridization

Introduction

One of the most frequently used terms in politics, and beyond, in recent years is undoubtedly "governance." Without delving too deeply into its origins and evolution, governance can be generally understood as referring to how a particular activity is directed or managed. This concept can apply to various areas; for example, there is "urban governance," which refers to how an urban center is organized and administered; there is also "corporate governance," which reflects how a company is managed, including how its goals and mission are achieved (Petrone, 2021a). These are just two examples of the many applications of this term.

Alongside these examples, there is also *global governance*, which refers to how international affairs are managed—specifically, what decisions are made and, more importantly, how they are made on issues that affect the entire planet. These matters are discussed in certain contexts (international forums) where representatives from nearly all the countries of the world participate. Hence, we can say that global governance is deeply linked to the institutions where these decisions, impacting humanity, are made. This includes international institutions such as the United Nations (UN), which, as we will describe, faces certain limitations that give rise to ongoing debates with no clear solutions.

It's also important to mention that, alongside international institutions like the UN, there are regional institutions such as the EU, MERCOSUR, ASEAN, and regional banks like the already mentioned NDB of the

BRICS. These regional organizations play a crucial role in global processes, particularly when it comes to decisions that affect specific regions and also have repercussions for the rest of the world. However, the contexts in which participation is broader are represented by international institutions, and therefore, our analysis primarily focuses on these.

To summarize, global governance refers to the manner in which decisions are made at the international level. This process involves not only the various countries but also a wide range of organizations—both governmental and non-governmental—and other non-state actors who are involved in the mechanism in one way or another.[1] Global governance, therefore, represents the collection of all these decision-making interactions that should lead to shared decisions. Above all, in recent decades, the decision-making system has sought, at least in theory, to ensure greater inclusivity for those countries that, due to their limited diplomatic and economic weight or low demographic indices, have historically been given little to no consideration in these processes.

To illustrate this point, we can reference the well-known definition of global governance from the *Commission on Global Governance* (1995, p. 2): "…the sum of many ways individuals and institutions, public and private, manage their common affairs. It is a continuing process through which conflicting or diverse interests may be accommodated and co-operative action taken. It includes formal institutions and regimes empowered to enforce compliance, as well as informal arrangements that people and institutions either have agreed to or perceive to be in their interest."

Therefore, based on these words, we can clearly understand how, in theory, this concept describes a decision-making process that should involve a wide range of actors, not just States. And this is the reality we live in today: issues such as climate change, but also migration, terrorism, and wars, require greater involvement from more actors precisely because they affect everyone.

However, at this point, despite the good intentions, the main criticisms of this concept and its practice also begin. Regarding conceptual criticisms, we can certainly mention the fact that, according to some scholars

[1] For example, for Rosenau (2009), these actors include NGOs, social movements, regions (both micro and macro), and municipalities (cities), states (referred to as 'issuing regimes'), transnational associations, rating agencies, interstate or international courts, the UN and the EU, as well as institutional mechanisms such as electoral observers. Each of these actors represents a sector that is made up of many other internal actors (e.g., there are many NGOs that pursue different objectives from one another).

(Friedrichs, 2009), the use of this English-origin term represents a kind of linguistic colonialism by academia, but also by Anglophone politics: the use of a term that was practically coined by English and/or American academia would conceal dark aspects that, at the same time, also make its application obscure. In short, these authors wonder if behind the use of this expression there is some hegemonic plot by Anglo-Saxon countries. In this regard, if we take the Italian language as an example, we can notice how the increase of English vocabulary certainly does not help in this regard. In Italian, for example, the term "governance" is not translated. In some other languages, it is translated, such as in Spanish (gobernanza) or in French (gouvernance), but as we can notice, the phoneme remains very similar to the original in English.

The Call for Reform of the International Monetary Fund, the World Bank, and the United Nations Security Council

Beyond epistemic disputes, however, in this chapter we are interested in analyzing the BRICS' view on global governance and international institutions. According to these countries, global governance must be reformed, and they are actively working to reshape it across various domains (Kirton & Larionova, 2018). Since the first summit in Ekaterinburg, one of the main points that the BRICS have been demanding is precisely a modification in the functioning of decision-making processes, with particular emphasis on financial institutions and the need to give more voice to the poorer countries in international forums, that is, those from the Global South (BRIC, 2009). At the following summit, held in Brasilia in 2010, the then BRIC countries dedicated the first point of the final declaration to their request for the transformation of global governance, stating: "We share the perception that the world is undergoing major and swift changes that highlight the need for corresponding transformations in global governance in all relevant areas" (BRIC, 2010).

Thus, in the view of the BRICS countries, global governance faces a fundamental paradox: although it is presented as an inclusive system that should encompass a wide range of actors, in practice it is still largely dominated by the most powerful countries and major international institutions. This phenomenon is reflected in the power dynamics within institutions such as the UN, the IMF, and the World Bank, where Global South countries, although formally represented, often lack real influence over decision-making. Global governance is not truly inclusive, as key decisions tend to be made by a small group of countries and actors who have the resources, political influence, and economic power to prevail in discussions and negotiations.

Moreover, another critical point is the lack of coherence and effectiveness in the decisions made, as many times global governance initiatives are merely recommendations or principles without effective implementation. This creates a gap between the theory of global governance and its practice, as the grand promises of inclusivity and joint action do not always translate into concrete policies that can solve the issues addressed in these forums.

In any case, in all the following summits after Brasilia, the reference to the reform of global governance is always present. But why do the BRICS speak of a reform of global governance? And, above all, why do they want a reform of global governance?

As we have briefly mentioned above, the main problem, according to them, is that global governance does not reflect the new reality that characterizes the contemporary world. To be more precise, from their point of view, the places where global decisions are made do not represent the will of many countries around the world and, therefore, do not reflect the presence of new powers that claim the right to have a greater voice in international matters. In the past, the international system was mainly supported as a pro-Western system, reflecting the interests and perspectives of the US and Western Europe. If we go back in history, to the period after World War II, the birth of international institutions, that is, the aforementioned Bretton Woods institutions (let us remember: the IMF, the World Bank, and the WTO, which was initially called GATT), marked the beginning of a period of greater influence and predominant presence of Western countries within these very institutions. Even the United Nations, according to them, is actually more controlled by these countries. We will talk about the UN in the next paragraph, but as for the Bretton Woods financial institutions, which are also defined as global governance institutions, these have primarily represented Western interests from the beginning. For example, as we will analyze in the next paragraph, the greater influence these countries have within these organizations is also reflected in their greater voting power.

IMF and World Bank Reform Attempts: Power Redistribution and Institutional Legitimacy

Since the end of World War II, the international monetary system has been structured around the IMF and the World Bank. As mentioned, these two institutions were established at Bretton Woods and were long dominated by Western powers. The US has consistently maintained a voting share sufficient to exercise veto power over key decisions, while European countries have acted as a cohesive bloc, reinforcing their collective influence. This power configuration was formalized through a tacit political arrangement: the IMF's Managing Director would always be a European, and the World Bank's President an American. This institutionalized hierarchy ensured the continuity of Western control and the preservation of a post-war liberal order centered on US economic leadership (Wade & Vestergaard, 2024). The reform initiatives launched in 2010 represented a critical moment in the longstanding debate over power redistribution within the Bretton Woods institutions. Under pressure from emerging economies—particularly the BRICS—the IMF's 14th General Review of Quotas called for a reallocation of 6% of total voting shares toward emerging and developing countries (EMDCs). This adjustment was meant to reflect the shifting balance of global economic power, positioning Brazil, Russia, India, and China among the IMF's top ten shareholders. However, since the reform required an 85% majority to enter into force, the US retained an effective veto over its implementation (International Monetary Fund, 2010).

In parallel, the World Bank agreed to a 4.59% transfer of voting power to EMDCs, the creation of a third Executive Director seat for Sub-Saharan Africa, and a commitment to five-yearly shareholding reviews designed to align voting weights with real economic performance. Yet, as Wade and Vestergaard (2024) demonstrate, these adjustments produced only minimal redistributive effects: between 2010 and 2020, developing countries gained a net total of merely 0.21 percentage points in voting power. The structural asymmetry in decision-making—anchored in preemptive rights, informal coordination among G7 members, and the persistent dominance of US and European interests—remained virtually untouched.

The institutional inertia that followed was particularly evident in the delayed implementation of the 2010 IMF reforms. The US Congress' refusal to ratify the changes until 2016 not only stalled the redistribution process but also eroded the institutional legitimacy of both the IMF and the World Bank in the eyes of the Global South. The partial entry into force of the reforms—symbolized by the inclusion of the Chinese renminbi (RMB) in the IMF's Special Drawing Rights basket—failed to substantively alter the global financial hierarchy. Similarly, the World Bank's 2015 shareholding review, which modestly increased China's voting power by 1.26 percentage points, did not challenge Western control. These limited reforms illustrate what Wade and Vestergaard (2024) call the "theatrics of inclusion": symbolic gestures designed to preserve legitimacy without redistributing authority. In this sense, global governance reform has functioned less as a mechanism of institutional adaptation and more as a strategy of status quo management, aimed at maintaining the credibility of institutions whose representational basis no longer mirrors the current geopolitical economy.

Facing this enduring imbalance, as we have previously described, the BRICS gradually shifted from a reformist to a revisionist stance, arguing that the Bretton Woods institutions risked obsolescence without genuine reform (BRICS, 2012). The creation of the NDB and the CRA marked a paradigmatic transition: from diplomatic pressure to the construction of parallel mechanisms of global financial governance. These initiatives sought not only to address short-term liquidity needs but also to embody an alternative normative vision of development financing—one premised on mutual sovereignty, policy autonomy, and South–South solidarity.

In analytical terms, the 2010 reform process highlights the structural limits of power redistribution within highly institutionalized regimes. Despite periodic commitments to representational balance, the IMF and World Bank remain embedded in a normative hierarchy that privileges the political and economic interests of the Global North. As such, reform has served to reaffirm, rather than transcend, the LIO's asymmetries. The persistence of this imbalance continues to undermine the institutional legitimacy of the Bretton Woods system, while simultaneously legitimizing alternative platforms—such as the NDB—that aspire to a more plural and multipolar form of global economic governance.

In fact, to assess the current situation and gain a clear understanding of the distribution of voting power, one can simply consult the IMF's website (International Monetary Fund, n.d.), which provides a detailed ranking of the voting system today. Indeed, it can be noted that while the US holds a voting share of 16.49%—enough to exercise veto power—the BRICS countries combined account for less than 15%. In general, the voting power of the countries of the Global North, led by the US, is nearly nine times greater than that of the Global South (Tricontinental, 2025). This imbalance has rightly sparked criticism regarding the legitimacy and fairness of the decisions taken within the IMF. If, instead, we compare this share with that of the NDB, we note that each of the five founding BRICS members holds a voting share of 20%.

A similar pattern emerges within the World Bank, where the distribution of voting rights continues to reflect a pronounced imbalance between the Global North and the Global South. The US holds approximately 15.8% of the votes in the International Bank for Reconstruction and Development (one of the five institutions that constitute the World Bank Group) and a significant quota share in the other institutions of the World Bank Group as well (World Bank, 2025), a share that not only consolidates its position as the Bank's largest shareholder but also grants it an effective veto power over major decisions, such as amendments to the Articles of Agreement, which require an 85% supermajority. The US remains the only country surpassing the 15% threshold and is therefore uniquely positioned to exercise this blocking power (Nelson, 2025). This configuration reinforces a governance structure in which the Global North, through the weight of advanced economies, maintains a disproportionate degree of influence, while the Global South—despite representing the majority of member states—holds comparatively limited voting shares and is consequently marginalized in the institution's decision-making processes.

Critics of the World Bank and the IMF therefore point out imbalances in governance, where the voting shares favor the wealthier nations—especially the Western ones—based on economic size and market openness, leaving the poorer countries that receive loans underrepresented. As for the IMF, despite the 2016 reforms that slightly increased China's influence, the voting power remains imbalanced in favor of the US, Europe, and Japan, with the US maintaining the right of veto over various key issues. At the World Bank, civil society organizations promote reforms such as double majority voting to strengthen the role of developing countries in decision-making processes (*Financial Times*, 2024). Despite some timid initiatives, the substance has changed little: it is the Western countries that maintain greater privileges and, therefore, also a greater decision-making capacity. On the other hand, during crises such as the one in 2008, the IMF's role was predominant in response to loan requests from struggling countries. And even in those instances, many criticized the danger of borrowing these funds, as it would have created greater dependence due to the incurred debts. Therefore, on this point, the group disagrees with the decision-making system of institutions like the IMF (Cohen, 2023). Consequently, they have already proposed reforming the voting system to reflect the changed world and their growing economic power within it (BRICS, 2023).

Thus, in this context, the issue becomes clearer. The BRICS are claiming a greater voice in these institutions. In fact, even though they have created the NDB and the CRA, these countries have not abandoned the Bretton Woods institutions. The reason is that they precisely want to have a say in these forums as well and, therefore, participate, especially nowadays, when they have greater diplomatic and economic capabilities, with more influence on international decisions, particularly in the financial sphere. Let us remember that these institutions have been criticized numerous times for their performance, and especially for implementing neoliberal financial strategies, in line with those of Western countries (Stiglitz, 2002). If we examine the operational performance of the NDB and the IMF side by side, we observe that since its establishment in 2015, the NDB has approved over 90 projects totaling around USD 32 billion (New Development Bank, 2025), with a strong emphasis on sustainable infrastructure, transport, and renewable energy, and without the stringent conditions typically associated with IMF loans (Shi, 2022). By contrast, although IMF lending over the period 2015–2025 has been considerably higher due to the Fund's much broader membership (International Monetary Fund, 2024), in practice these loans have been predominantly directed toward short-term bailouts tied to structural conditionality (Krahnke, 2023; Pazarbasioglu, 2023). This comparison highlights how the NDB seeks to position itself as a complementary source of financing with fewer strings attached, reflecting the BRICS' ambition to reduce the dominance of Bretton Woods institutions, both in terms of access to loans and in terms of loan management and the strict conditions required to obtain them.

However, as mentioned earlier, these institutions, as well as the decision-making processes that characterize them, do not reflect the changed world that sees the rise of these countries as increasingly central players in international relations. In practice, the main criticism that the BRICS make of global governance is that it is a reflection of an outdated world, a world that reflects the post-World War II structure, and that has not yet adopted new forms of inclusion and participation in decision-making processes, which should be adopted, first and foremost, because the countries that have increased their diplomatic and economic weight (among them, the BRICS themselves) have grown; and then because global problems require global responses that involve the participation of a wider range of actors in decision-making processes. For example, and this is a topic we will address in more detail in the chapter dedicated to the Global South countries, the BRICS also demand that the voice of the Global South be placed at the center of the international agenda, meaning they demand greater prominence for these Southern countries, in which, moreover, issues like climate change and poverty have a greater and more devastating impact (Ngcamu, 2023).

The Reform of the United Nations Security Council: Reality or Rhetoric?

One of the main reasons that has favored the formation and growth of the BRICS has undoubtedly been their increasing economic power. To this, we must add the abovementioned desire to reform both international institutions, particularly those of Bretton Woods, and, more generally, global financial governance. Moreover, one of their claims is to place the issues of the Global South at the center of the international agenda, the latter often systematically ignored, according to them, in forums led and dominated primarily by Western powers. From this perspective, the will of some members of the group to reform the UN system must also be considered. Although in their official statements, the group repeatedly affirms the importance of maintaining the centrality of the UN within global governance, Brazil, India, and South Africa support a reform of the UN system, particularly of the Security Council, of which China and Russia are already members. To be more precise, Brazil argues that South America is not represented in the Security Council, and as the largest power in the region, it aspires to a seat on that Council. South Africa's motivations are similar to those of Brazil, considering that Africa also lacks representation in the Security Council. India, for its part, calls for a reform of the Security Council due to its growing power and to play a more decisive role in the international system. Furthermore, India and Brazil are also part of the so-called Group of Four (G4), which represents a group of countries that claim a permanent seat on the UN Security Council. In fact, the G4, composed of Germany, Brazil, India, and Japan, argues that the current organization of the Security Council is anachronistic. The G4 calls for an expansion of the Security Council, as a Council with only five permanent members and such a conditioning veto power could also represent an obstacle to resolutions of general interest, such as climate change and nuclear proliferation. In summary, the five permanent members could (as has indeed happened on several occasions) frequently use their veto power to promote their own national interests and will. China and Russia are already permanent members of the Security Council, but they have supported—at least in theory—these requests for an expansion of the Council from the other BRICS members (Petrone, 2021b). However, as can be observed, contradictions remain. While BRICS collectively call for a more representative and democratic global governance system, China and Russia already enjoy permanent seats and veto rights on the UN Security Council, making their support for reform appear selective. BRICS have consistently advocated expanding the Council to include India, Brazil, and South Africa, thereby enhancing Global South representation. Yet progress has stalled, partly due to China's reluctance to support India's candidacy and Russia's preference for gradual reform. This paradox—demanding democratization while defending existing privileges—underscores the inherent tensions in the BRICS' reformist discourse and may hinder their ability to effect meaningful change in global governance structures (*Financial Times*, 2025).

These mechanisms are important as they indicate a widespread dissatisfaction with one of the institutions symbolically created after the tragedies of the two world wars of the last century. However, this issue raises a more general problem, namely, the need to reform the UN, which appears stagnant and outdated.

BRICS and the EU: Two Different Views and Approaches to Global Governance

The challenges facing the world are of crucial importance, which is why it is essential to understand the role that various countries can play in the future. Since this is of particular interest to us, we believe it is interesting to draw a parallel with the EU. In fact, the EU can serve as an example to understand the different visions that the BRICS have about global governance and, in general, about multilateralism. Moreover, the rise of the BRICS, as well as the internal dynamics of the Union itself, havs led to a crisis in the very initial European project. All these factors are having significant impacts on international dynamics. In particular, while on one hand the EU is undergoing a major crisis, and in a certain sense its project, although not finished, seems quite undermined in its foundations, on the other hand, the BRICS embody a different vision of global governance that seems, at least for now, more successful and, above all, presents a potential to attract new partner countries to the group.

The EU, which among the pillars of its mission declares multilateralism as a fundamental element for global policies, is now facing emerging powers claiming a more relevant role in international matters and to which it must respond clearly, multilaterally, and collaboratively, considering the urgent issues we have previously outlined. The EU represents a group of countries that have managed to unify after centuries of wars, demonstrating an inclination to defend multilateralism. In this sense, this project assigns to its structure and its initial essence an unmistakable tendency toward multilateralism. In our view, the element of multilateralism is indispensable in the contemporary era for various reasons. First, the rise of new emerging powers like the BRICS implies a shift in the international order and a different direction that globalization is taking. Second, humanity is facing significant problems that require global coordination to find effective solutions. Just think about the climate issue, one of the most relevant problems we are currently facing. This is just one example of the approach to global issues related to global governance. In fact, to make distinctions and comparisons at the same time, we can notice how the EU's vision of multilateralism offers a different perspective compared to that of the BRICS (Petrone, 2025).

The EU seeks to establish binding rules governing international affairs. This approach is embodied in the concept of *effective multilateralism*, which emphasizes legally binding commitments and robust international regimes as both the outcomes and instruments of multilateral cooperation. For the EU, these rules should extend beyond economic and political relations to include other policy areas—such as environmental and social issues—as well as the internal governance of member states, including respect for human rights and the rule of law (Hooijmaaijers & Keukeleire, 2014).

In practice, in their mission, the countries of the EU also include binding and legally established commitments. This issue, which is also evident in what is called the "acquis communautaire," that is, the stages and commitments that members wishing to join the Union must fulfill to be admitted to the group, represents a key point that differentiates the EU from the BRICS. In fact, the latter see binding rules as obstacles to their growth and their right to pursue a development model suited to their needs.

Indeed, when analyzing the various alliances of emerging powers and the multilateral frameworks in the Asia-Pacific region, it becomes clear that Asian countries and other emerging powers have also embraced multilateralism—as Europeans have—but they have done so by embracing fundamentally different principles. In terms of content, they prioritize economic growth and development, with a reluctance to allow the economy to be limited by concerns that Europeans consider important, such as social protection or human rights. They have a clear preference for a purely intergovernmental approach: decisions made by consensus, absence of contractual obligations, voluntary commitments, and respect for national sovereignty (Hooijmaaijers & Keukeleire, 2014). It is evident that, in this context, the different visions of multilateralism between the two parties have a decisive impact on global governance, highlighting their various limitations. Furthermore, we find it interesting to underline the different perspectives that the EU and the BRICS have on the issue of sovereignty. While the EU's normative power is used to influence the national policies of countries (from its members and those applying to join the group), the BRICS affirm the principle of sovereignty. In fact, each admission to the BRICS group is not conditioned by issues related to changes in the political, social, or economic structure of the countries (as is the case in the EU's enlargement policies), but by mutual benefit, especially in commercial and economic terms.

It is also important to recall the EU's enduring Atlantic orientation, which continues to shape its foreign policy. The Union remains dependent—particularly in military terms—as most member states are also members of NATO, a factor that complicates European security and often generates internal tensions. NATO membership has long been a key source of friction within the EU, constraining its capacity to attain genuine strategic autonomy in defense. During the Cold War, Atlantic solidarity and European integration were frequently viewed as mutually exclusive in matters of security. The combination of US military dominance, European weakness, and the perceived Soviet threat made dependence on American protection a necessary condition for the Union's stability (Delreux & Keukeleire, 2014).

At the same time, this dependence on NATO appears difficult to overcome. The EU has repeatedly underscored the indispensability of its cooperation with NATO, particularly during the recent war between Russia and Ukraine (European Council, 2023). Although some tentative efforts were made to advance the idea of "strategic autonomy" during the 2021 European Council summit, the final declaration promptly clarified that:

> We are committed to cooperating closely with NATO, in full respect of the principles set out in the Treaties and those agreed by the European Council [...]. (European Council, 2021 p. 4)

These elements, although they only represent a summary of the problems the EU must face, outline a clear picture. The Union is affected by various crises, a strong dependence on the US (especially in terms of security, but also in other areas, including political approach), and a limited ability to engage in constructive dialogue with the new emerging powers. However, despite the crisis, the EU could still play a key role in the future of global governance. In this context, the recent re-election of Trump—who has shifted his stance toward NATO and Europe, even calling European allies "parasites" (A2 News, 2025) demanding substantial contributions to defense as part of the NATO alliance, and successfully securing an agreement for member countries to increase their defense spending to 5% of GDP by 2035 (Associated Press, 2025; Cienski, 2025)—may, at some point, push the EU to develop alternative defense strategies. In this regard, recent trends of increasing military spending and a stronger hard-power approach within the EU appear to move in that direction (European Council, 2025).

In our view, greater openness in terms of strategic partnerships, on the part of the EU, toward emerging (or already emerged) powers like the BRICS could be decisive for the future of global governance, but also for the future of the Union itself. A series of measures aimed at making the EU more open to new challenges and more cohesive and autonomous could represent a turning point for the future of this project, which, although in need of reforms, represents an important achievement for humanity. At the same time, rather than seeing it as a purely contrasting relationship, we believe that the interactions between the EU and the BRICS should be interpreted as a process of hybridization. Instead of viewing the traditional dichotomy between Western liberal governance and the state-centric or authoritarian approaches associated with other Non-Western countries (such as the BRICS) as mutually exclusive, these models should be understood as elements of a dynamic process within a more inclusive framework of global governance. Our perspective suggests that global institutions and practices do not emerge from a single normative paradigm, but rather from the interaction and mutual influence of diverse models—both Western and non-Western—leading to the creation of new, more inclusive, and adaptable institutional configurations.

References

A2 News. (2025, March 26). Trump backs Vance's talk: Europe is a parasite! 'When will EU leaders act?'. Retrieved October 24, 2025, from https://a2news.com/english/rajoni-bota/bota/trump-mbeshtet-biseden-e-vance-evropa-eshte-nje-parazit-kur-do-i1143788

Associated Press. (2025, June 05). NATO is on the cusp of accepting Trump's 5% defense investment demand, Rutte says. https://apnews.com/article/nato-capability-targets-plans-defense-spending-trump-b123977c8f3c1bce277fb1b9957b1b78

BRIC Leaders Meeting. (2009, January 16). The 1st BRIC Summit: Yekaterinburg Declaration, Russia. http://en.kremlin.ru/supplement/209

BRIC Leaders Meeting. (2010, April 15). The 2nd BRICS Summit: Brasília Declaration, Brazil. http://www.brics.utoronto.ca/docs/100415-leaders.html

BRICS Leaders Meeting. (2012, March 29). The 4th BRICS Summit, Delhi Declaration. https://www.mea.gov.in/bilateral-documents.htm?dtl/19158/

BRICS Leaders Meeting. (2023, August 23). The 15th BRICS Summit: Johannesburg II Declaration. *BRICS and Africa: "Partnership for Mutually Accelerated Growth, Sustainable Development and Inclusive Multilateralism"*, Sandton, Gauteng, South Africa

Cienski, J. (2025, June 22). NATO allies agree to 5 percent defense spending goal. *Politico*. https://www.politico.eu/article/nato-allies-defense-spending-goal-spain-gdp/

Cohen, T. (2023, August 21). After the Bell: IMF voting power doesn't reflect what the BRICS countries claim. *Daily Maverick*. https://www.dailymaverick.co.za/article/2023-08-21-after-the-bell-imf-voting-power-doesnt-reflect-what-the-brics-countries-claim/

Commission on Global Governance. (1995). *Our global neighborhood*. Oxford University Press.

Delreux, T., & Keukeleire, S. (2014). *The Foreign Policy of the European Union* (2nd ed.). Palgrave Macmillan.

European Council. (2021). *Statement of the members of the European Council, 25-26 February 2021*, Brussels. https://www.consilium.europa.eu/media/48625/2526-02-21-euco-statement-en.pdf

European Council. (2023). *EU-NATO cooperation*. https://www.consilium.europa.eu/en/policies/defence-security/eu-nato-cooperation/

European Council. (2025, September 01). *Keynote speech by President António Costa at the opening of the Bled Strategic Forum.* https://www.consilium.europa.eu/en/press/press-releases/2025/09/01/keynote-speech-by-president-antonio-costa-at-the-opening-of-the-bled-strategic-forum/

Financial Times. (2024, October 18). Why the World Bank and IMF matter more than ever. https://www.ft.com/content/0dce48c3-e203-4f90-ab9f-d80b824e0685

Financial Times. (2025, July 09). The Brics lose their clout. https://www.ft.com/content/e2b3392f-ac37-44e3-b86c-5c2ecbaa192f

Friedrichs, J. (2009). Global governance as liberal hegemony. In J. Whitman (Ed.), *Palgrave advances in global governance*. Palgrave Macmillan. https://doi.org/10.1057/9780230245310_6

Hooijmaaijers, B., & Keukeleire, S. (2014). The BRICS and other emerging power alliances and multilateral organizations in the Asia-Pacific and the Global South: Challenges for the European Union and Its View on Multilateralism. *Journal of Common Market Studies, 52*(3), 582–599. https://doi.org/10.1111/jcms.12102

International Monetary Fund. (2010, November 5). IMF survey: IMF board approves far-reaching governance reforms. https://www.imf.org/en/News/Articles/2015/09/28/04/53/sonew110510b.

International Monetary Fund. (2024). Lending. In IMF Annual Report 2024. https://www.imf.org/external/pubs/ft/ar/2024/what-we-do/lending/

International Monetary Fund. (n.d.). Member's quota and voting power. Retrieved October 24, 2025, from https://www.imf.org/en/About/executive-board/members-quotas

Kirton, J., & Larionova, M. (Eds.). (2018). *BRICS and global governance*. Routledge.

Krahnke, T. (2023). Doing more with less: The catalytic function of IMF lending and the role of program size. *Journal of International Money and Finance, 135*, 102856. https://doi.org/10.1016/j.jimonfin.2023.102856

Nelson, R. M. (2025). The World Bank (CRS In Focus IF11361). Congressional Research Service. https://www.congress.gov/crs-product/IF11361

New Development Bank. (2025). All projects. Retrieved September 25, 2025, from https://www.ndb.int/projects/all-projects/

Ngcamu, B. S. (2023). Climate change effects on vulnerable populations in the Global South: A systematic review. *Nat Hazards, 118*, 977–991. https://doi.org/10.1007/s11069-023-06070-2

Pazarbasioglu, C. (2023, October 9). Why IMF lending continues to adapt. International Monetary Fund. https://www.imf.org/en/Blogs/Articles/2023/10/09/why-imf-lending-continues-to-adapt

Petrone, F. (2021a). *Globalizzazione, Governance e Istituzioni Internaizonali*. Aracne.

Petrone, F. (2025). The European Union, the BRICS Countries, and the Global South: Rethinking Multilateralism and Global Governance in a Time of Polycrisis. *International Critical Thought, 15*(3), 419–436. https://doi.org/10.1080/21598282.2025.2554499

Petrone, F. (2021b). BRICS and global governance: Will the grouping be able to reform the United Nations Security Council? *International Studies, 58*(3), 363–379. https://doi.org/10.1177/00208817211029409

Rosenau, J. (2009). Governance in the twenty-first century. In J. Whitman (Ed.), *Global governance*. Palgrave Macmillan.

Shi, J. (2022, October 26). NDB underlines funding for green areas. *China Daily*.

Stiglitz, J. E. (2002). *Globalization and its discontents*. Penguin.

Tricontinental: Institute for Social Research. (2025, March 6). The Global North Has Nine Times More Voting Power at the IMF Than the Global South: The Tenth Newsletter. https://thetricontinental.org/newsletterissue/global-north-imf-inequality/.

Wade, R. H., & Vestergaard, J. (2024, September 23). World Bank governance reform: 'Puppet on a string?'. *Global Policy*. https://www.globalpolicyjournal.com/blog/23/09/2024/world-bank-governance-reform-puppet-string

World Bank. (2025). Voting powers. World Bank. Retrieved September 25, 2025, from https://www.worldbank.org/en/about/leadership/votingpowers

CHAPTER 4

New World Order and Multipolarity

Abstract The contemporary international system is undergoing a profound transformation, marked by the decline of US hegemony and the emergence of a multipolar—or, as Amitav Acharya terms it, "multiplex"—world order. While scholars from both the Global North and South have identified this transition as the end of the Pax Americana, the contours of the new global order remain uncertain, reflecting an interregnum in Gramsci's sense: a period in which the old order is fading and the new one has yet to fully emerge. Within this evolving landscape, the rise of the BRICS and their BRICS Plus strategy has become a defining feature of twenty-fir-century geopolitics, challenging Western dominance and contributing to a more plural, balanced system of governance. This chapter contrasts three classical configurations of world order—bipolarity, unipolarity, and multipolarity—highlighting how the post-Cold War "unipolar moment" has given way to a more diffuse and complex structure. Multipolarity, characterized by multiple centers of power, offers the potential for more inclusive and representative decision-making but also introduces new uncertainties, as dialogue among these centers remains fragile. The multiplex perspective deepens this analysis by emphasizing not only the diffusion of power but also the coexistence of multiple modernities, narratives, and governance models, reflecting a shift from a single liberal international order to overlapping regional and normative systems. The expansion of the BRICS through the BRICS Plus framework—most

F. Petrone, *The BRICS and the Transformation of Global Power*,
https://doi.org/10.1007/978-3-032-23540-4_4

recently including Egypt, Iran, the United Arab Emirates, Ethiopia, and Indonesia—embodies this transformation, promoting South–South cooperation and new financial architectures such as the New Development Bank and the Contingent Reserve Arrangement. Meanwhile, the relative decline of the G7 and the strategic relevance of the G20 illustrate how traditional Western-led forums are being complemented—and, at times, contested—by emerging multilateral platforms. Together, these developments signal a reconfiguration of global governance toward a more polycentric, plural, and contested order, in which the BRICS play a pivotal role as both architects and symbols of a post-hegemonic world.

Keywords Multipolarity • Multiplex World • BRICS Plus • Global Governance • G7 and G20 • Post-Hegemonic Order

Introduction

Scholars from the Global South, but also from the North, have attempted to find an appropriate definition for this period, which they see as marking the end of US hegemony—already evident in their view—and the emergence of a new world order. Regarding this new world order, some authors have coined expressions that, while aiming to indicate that the world is in a phase of transformation or transition, essentially highlight that the new world order is still very much *in fieri*. This means that there are still no sufficient analytical or practical elements for an effective and comprehensive description of its essential characteristics. To cite just a few examples, we can mention authors such as Amitav Acharya (2014), Kishore Mahbubani (2009), Oliver Stuenkel (2016), and Fareed Zakaria (2008).

All these authors share the idea that the world under US leadership is in decline, and that a new phase is emerging in international relations and, more broadly, in the global order. In many respects, the current epilogue to the so-called *Pax Americana* (Holzner, 2024) was predictable. Across the world, US interventions in issues of international concern—though officially justified by humanitarian motives and a declared commitment to "exporting democracy"—have often been perceived as intrusions into the internal affairs of other states, thereby undermining their sovereignty and aggravating pre-existing conflicts. The recent turn toward tariff-based and isolationist policies in the US can thus be interpreted as an attempt to preserve the last vestiges of its hegemonic position through coercive means—an approach that, in the long term, may ultimately prove counterproductive.

Obviously, this decline is not due solely to geopolitical issues, but stems from a broader matrix that transcends an intrinsic inability on the part of the US-led system to manage global issues—issues that require a global effort, or at least a different approach from the one implemented thus far under the banner of stars and stripes. We will discuss this point further later on. For now, however, we wish to offer a reflection on this world in transition, a phase of decline highlighted by the authors mentioned, even though they are not yet able to describe what kind of international order will emerge in the future. In our view, this period can be described as an interregnum—a transitional phase in which the old order is fading while the new one has yet to emerge, giving rise to numerous troubling and uncertain phenomena, as the italian philosopher Antonio Gramsci once observed (Gramsci, 2014).

Thus, the era we are living in represents a moment of suspension in history, and we still lack the means to understand what future order will eventually emerge. However, even though the moment is so uncertain, what certainly demands particular attention—and possibly timely interventions—are all those global issues already mentioned that characterize our time: from climate change to migration, from the spread of terrorism to wars. In short, while the world navigates this period, serious threats loom over it.

In line with the rise of the BRICS and their BRICS Plus strategy, the current moment could either signal a turning point or slide into disorder. By "disorder," we mean a world growing more anarchic and leaderless, as global challenges become harder to manage. Much will depend on how relations with these countries are structured. The EU, for instance, has not established direct ties with the BRICS as a group but instead maintains individual "strategic partnerships" with each member (Petrone, 2025). Rather than acknowledging the bloc's collective reality and fostering dialogue on shared issues, this fragmented approach raises doubts. Relations with Russia remain strained due to the war in Ukraine, and the recent election of Trump has deepened the EU's uncertainty. Under the previous US administration, transatlantic alignment was clearer; now, faced with new tariffs and Washington's unilateral approach to Ukraine, the EU's limitations are increasingly evident—especially given internal divisions, such as Hungary's opposition to sanctions on Russia.

Another example is the EU's relationship with China, where the 27 member states struggle to adopt a unified stance. Each tends to pursue its own strategic interests: Italy, for instance, has recently withdrawn from the Belt and Road Initiative (BRI), while several Eastern European countries have embraced it enthusiastically and maintain close cooperation with Beijing (Kaufmann & Sielker, 2020), based on the principle of economic complementarity with China and the long-term potential of market development and geographical advantages (Smotrytska, 2020).

These examples clearly illustrate the complexity of EU–BRICS relations. They reveal two key points: first, the need for genuine dialogue with the increasingly expanding group; and second, the importance of strengthening the EU's "strategic autonomy," enabling it to act independently toward partners whose positions may shift unexpectedly. Beyond these relational dynamics, what stands out is the absence of a single power center and the emergence of multiple ones—an era of multipolarity whose nature remains uncertain.

Indeed, multiple centers of power now exist—but what does this imply? Are we entering a phase of global disorder or even "anarchy," a concept long used in political theory to describe relations among states (Waltz, 1979)? After World War II, the international structure appeared relatively clear: a bipolar system dominated by the US and the Soviet Union, competing for global influence across political, economic, and cultural spheres. With the Soviet collapse, described by Fukuyama's notion of the "End of History" (Fukuyama, 1992), this gave way to a "unipolar moment" (Krauthammer, 2002) during which the US and its European allies stood as unrivaled powers, marked by American economic dominance and its global influence—exercised through both soft and hard power.

Although thinkers like Fukuyama proclaimed the "end of history," suggesting that the liberal model—based on democracy, freedom, and economic growth—had prevailed, the crises that have affected the Western world since the early 2000s have revealed its limits. The LIO, in its unilateral form, has proven unable to address today's economic, environmental, and security challenges. Meanwhile, the rise of the BRICS has asserted these countries' demand for greater influence in global affairs. As a result, the world is now better described as a multipolar system increasingly reflecting the BRICS' imprint—defined by multiple centers of power rather than a Western-dominated order (Andreoni & Casado, 2019).

However, while it is increasingly clear that today's world is polycentric, Western countries—especially those in the EU—lack the structures, mechanisms, and perhaps even the mindset to adapt to this reality. The traditional tools used to restrain emerging non-Western powers—the so-called Rest —are now outdated and largely ineffective. The case of sanctions on Russia, which have had limited impact, illustrates this well. Ultimately, the key question remains: Are we truly prepared to live in a multipolar world? In any case, to delve deeper, in the next paragraph we will focus on what the term multipolar specifically means, also referring back to the previously analyzed bipolar and unipolar systems.

Multipolarity, Bipolarity, and Unipolarity in Comparison

The term "multipolarity" describes an international system in which there are multiple centers of power and influence, none of which is able to dominate the others in an absolute manner. This concept has become increasingly relevant since the late twentieth century, when the global geopolitical structure underwent historic changes.

To fully understand multipolarity, it is helpful to analyze it in relation to other models of international order:

- **Bipolarity**: A bipolar system is when global power is divided between two superpowers, each leading a group of allies. The most emblematic case is the Cold War, in which the world was divided between the Western bloc led by the US and the Eastern bloc under Soviet influence.
- **Unipolarity**: The situation in which a single power dominates the international landscape. The most evident example is the period after the Cold War, when the US, without a true geopolitical rival, exerted dominant influence in the economic, military, and political spheres.
- **Multipolarity**: Unlike the previous two models, a multipolar system envisions the presence of more global actors with a relatively balanced level of power, preventing one nation from imposing its hegemony.

Unlike unipolarity, which risks leading to imbalances and unilateral decisions, multipolarity fosters greater dialogue among various actors, promoting solutions that are more shared and representative of global diversity. However, this aspect seems to be precisely what is least present in the current world, where there is a struggle to find a shared consensus. Indeed, a major contradiction of the contemporary world is precisely this: while we are, de facto, living in a multipolar world, dialogue between countries and among centers of power appears to be weakening. This trend, fueled by recent populist, conservative, and anti-globalization currents, risks generating unpredictable escalations, as exemplified by the war in Ukraine.

The Implications of Multipolarity in the Twenty-First Century

The transition to a multipolar world is not only a matter of balancing power, but also has deep implications in several areas:

- **Geopolitics and international security**: In a multipolar system, international security becomes more complex. There is no longer a single power capable of acting as the "global policeman," as was the case in the post-Cold War unipolar period with the US. This leads to greater balance among powers but also potential competition among different geopolitical blocs, such as the Euro-Atlantic, the BRICS, and emerging regional powers.
- **Global economy and (new) financial institutions**: One of the most visible aspects of multipolarity is the reduction of Western economic hegemony. While for decades financial institutions like the IMF and World Bank set the rules of the game, today entities such as the BRICS Bank (NDB) and the Asian Infrastructure Investment Bank (AIIB) offer concrete alternatives to emerging countries. This means that more and more nations can access financing and investments without necessarily adhering to the criteria imposed by Western-dominated institutions.
- **Global governance and multilateral diplomacy**: Multipolarity promotes a more inclusive approach to global governance, as we have seen in the dedicated chapter. Organisms such as the United Nations, or forums like the G20 and the BRICS, try to facilitate dialogue among diverse regions of the world, providing platforms for negotiating shared solutions to critical issues such as climate change, the regulation of artificial intelligence, and food security.

The Role of the BRICS in Building Multipolarity

The BRICS alliance is strengthening its position with the goal of rebalancing global power and offering developing countries greater opportunities for participation in international decision-making.

The BRICS initiatives to promote multipolarity (and multilateralism) include:

- The NDB, an alternative to the IMF
- The growing use of national currencies in trade exchanges, reducing dependence on the US dollar
- A strengthening of South–South cooperation, which promotes investment and infrastructure development in developing countries, without the traditional conditions imposed by Western institutions

With the expansion of the BRICS group and the admission of new members, this alliance could become increasingly influential, helping to consolidate a more stable and representative multipolar system. The BRICS are well aware of this and advocate for this new, more inclusive approach to international relations. For example, the XV BRICS Declaration, following the Johannesburg Summit (August 2023), in its Preamble states: "We reiterate our commitment to inclusive multilateralism and upholding international law, including the purposes and principles enshrined in the Charter of 2 the United Nations (UN) as its indispensable cornerstone, and the central role of the UN in an international system [...]" (BRICS, 2023).

Multipolarity therefore represents a fundamental step in the redefinition of the world order. It does not necessarily mean the end of Western influence, but rather the creation of a more balanced system in which different nations and regional blocs can play a significant role in global decisions. In practice, it is about recognizing that alongside the traditional Western hegemonic powers, new powers have emerged that have every right and capacity to exert their influence in the future world order. The turning point is precisely in this: in recognizing the growing importance and strategic potential of these countries and being willing to listen, in addition to expecting to be heard. It is useful to adopt a dichotomous perspective on multilateralism when comparing the approaches of the BRICS and Western countries. Western analyses of multipolarity often frame it in terms of instability, the decline of US hegemony, and potential systemic chaos. For instance, studies on the post-American world highlight the weakening of US-led institutions and growing geopolitical competition in regions such as the Indo-Pacific, where the US itself has sought to maintain its presence through the "Pivots' to Asia" policy (Cossa & Brad Glosserman, 2022; Kupchan, 2020; Ikenberry, 2018). In contrast, the BRICS emphasize institutional experimentation, cooperative development, and governance that respects national sovereignty. Initiatives such as the NDB and the CRA illustrate a concrete effort to shape a multipolar order. Where Western observers stress power vacuums and the risks of disorder, BRICS leaders frame multipolarity as an opportunity to reform global governance and amplify the voice of non-Western actors. This contrast highlights not only differing interpretations of global shifts but also divergent strategies for influencing the international order.

At the same time, significant internal asymmetries exist within the BRICS themselves. China's economic and geopolitical dominance, with a GDP of $18.74 trillion (World Bank, 2025) and a rapidly expanding Belt and Road network, contrasts sharply with the smaller economies and regional influence of India, Brazil, Russia, and South Africa. India's GDP of approximately $3.9 trillion, Brazil's $2.18 trillion, Russia's $2.17 trillion, and South Africa's approximately $0.40 trillion (World Bank, n.d.) underline the disparity in economic power, which raises questions about the sustainability of an egalitarian multipolar framework within the group. To mitigate these disparities, the BRICS employ institutional mechanisms such as the NDB's voting structure, the CRA's rotational governance, and the rotating BRICS presidency. These arrangements enable the group to present a coordinated front despite internal hierarchies, demonstrating that the BRICS approach to multipolarity is carefully negotiated, balancing asymmetries with institutional safeguards.

Multipolar or "Multiplex" World?

An additional interesting view, which aims to be more illustrative of the current international situation, is one that describes the present world as a "multiplex world" rather than multipolar. This definition, coined by Amitav Acharya, indicates a global order in which multiple narratives, economic approaches, and political visions coexist, overlapping and giving rise to networks of power and influence that compete with one another. More specifically, Acharya argues (2017) that the emerging world is not a multipolar world, but a multiple world, characterized by multiple modernities, among which the Western liberal modernity, with its patterns of economic development and governance, represents only one of the available options. In this context, the multiplex world is defined by interconnections and interdependencies, not by a single global order, whether liberal or of another kind, but by a complex set of international orders and globalisms that often overlap or compete.

In our view, although the terms "multipolarity" and "multiplex" are conceptually distinct, in practice they can be seen as converging toward a common *locus*: an international system characterized both by the existence of multiple centers of power (multipolarity) and by a plurality of narratives and worldviews (multiplex). In reality, given the most pressing challenges facing humanity, these dimensions could—and should—find ways to converge in shared policies, practices, and solutions. Thus, the two concepts may serve to envision a future in which hybrid institutions and practices emerge, giving rise to a form of hybrid global governance that moves beyond the particularistic and unilateral visions currently reinforcing gridlock within the international system.

However, at least for now Western countries appear to be struggling to adapt to this transformed international context. Often constrained by a Eurocentric perspective rooted in a colonial past, in which Europe and the US acted as aggressive conquerors under the self-justified myth of "civilizing the world" (Brolsma et al., 2019), Western states seem increasingly challenged by a global order marked by the gradual decline of their hegemony. In contrast, the BRICS, motivated by a desire for greater influence on the international stage and aware that they can potentially benefit from this period of "power transition" (Gilpin, 1981), are developing stronger institutional structures, diplomatic capacity, and strategic coordination. While their approach is certainly driven by national interests and still marked by internal contradictions among members, it also demonstrates a greater willingness to operate within—and actively shape—a multipolar world that they themselves are helping to construct.

The BRICS Plus Strategy

The BRICS represent one of the most significant diplomatic and geopolitical innovations of the past few years. The creation of the group aims to manage the transition to a new global order, which is increasingly centered in Asia, without causing drastic ruptures. The member countries play a key role in this process, contributing to the construction of a different international balance. Despite differences in terms of civilization, culture, and traditions, the BRICS countries have managed to find common ground and promote a debate on the future of the global order. Although some critics accuse the group of wanting to subvert the existing system, its strategy is actually more subtle: instead of demolishing current institutions, the BRICS work to reform them while also creating new ones, such as the aforementioned NDB, which provides additional global public goods, including credit and development financing.

In a context marked by the rising wave of protectionism and opposition to globalization, the BRICS assume a fundamental role in defending global economic integration, and in their approach, they try to avoid the mistakes of the past that led to conflicts. Globalization is not an option but an inevitable reality, and the task is to manage it in a sustainable and beneficial way for all.

After the global financial crisis of 2008, the BRICS economies have gone through phases of slowdown, with Brazil, South Africa, and Russia involved in a process of adapting to new economic conditions. However, India and China continue to grow, and the total weight of the bloc today is higher than initial forecasts. Despite criticisms claiming that the BRICS era has ended, the group maintains strategic relevance, and the connections between its members are set to strengthen in the coming years. The 2017 summit in Xiamen, China, considered a crucial moment for the future of the bloc, saw the proposal of the "BRICS Plus" initiative, aimed at fostering greater integration between emerging markets and developing countries (BRICS, 2017). This initiative is seen as an opportunity to make the BRICS group more inclusive and legitimized to represent the emerging world. Therefore, contrary to what many Western critics thought, the BRICS phenomenon is not destined to end anytime soon. On the contrary, it seems destined to grow even more. Proof of this is precisely the BRICS Plus strategy, which we will frequently reference in the various chapters, but to which we dedicate a specific analysis in this one.

In fact, the BRICS Plus strategy represents one of the most important points to describe the transition of the global order. In practice, the strategy embodies the emblem of this transforming world order, as well as the implementation, above all, of a strategy to include countries that otherwise had little prominence in any international forum. At the same time, the BRICS Plus strategy embodies a series of initiatives that will lead the group to have an increasingly significant weight on the international stage, thanks to the continuous entry of new countries and the request from many others to join the group. In several cases, some of these countries aspiring to join the group tend to be adversarial to Western countries, such as Cuba, Venezuela, or even Iran; or they are countries seeking to expand their strategic partnerships to participate in more forums and have more trade partners.

The initiative, therefore, not only comes at the right moment, as the BRICS seek new avenues for development, but it can also be considered one of the first true global initiatives from the developing world to shape a new, more balanced economic order, a multilateral diplomatic order, and, in general, a more inclusive global system. This is possible, among other things, thanks to the nature of the BRICS, represented by one or more major powers on nearly all continents of the developing world.

The BRICS Plus strategy represents, then, in concrete terms, a significant expansion of the BRICS group, originally composed of Brazil, Russia, India, China, and (then) South Africa. This expansion aims to strengthen cooperation and promote a more multipolar world order. Although some authors see this strategy primarily as an incentive for China to expand its spheres of influence and hegemony (Stuenkel, 2023), our impression is slightly different. While it is true that the expansion to new members undoubtedly offers new opportunities for trade partnerships and more, from a diplomatic standpoint, this opportunity allows new members to have greater participation in a forum that is increasingly gaining weight internationally, and enables the BRICS countries to position themselves as the true voice of the Global South. We will dedicate a specific chapter to this point, but in this chapter, it is important to highlight this aspect because it is crucial to emphasize how many countries of the Global South, which previously had little voice in international matters, can now find commercial and diplomatic avenues in this new group. It is also true that the expansion of the BRICS progressively increases the heterogeneity of the group, which raises the complexity of managing it. However, this process is, in some ways, inevitable and aligns with the BRICS strategy and its ambitions to gain increasing weight globally, especially in those regions of the world that until now have suffered a certain, if not total, exclusion from decision-making and global governance mechanisms. Furthermore, this expansion marks a fundamental step in history, putting an end to that period of unilateralism, also defined as Pax Americana, as mentioned (Holzner, 2024), and inaugurating a period in which multipolarity truly prevails.

Regarding the expansion process, more specifically, as of January 1, 2024, four new countries have joined the BRICS nations: Egypt, Ethiopia, Iran, and the United Arab Emirates. Saudi Arabia, although initially invited to officially join the group in 2024, postponed its accession until 2025. At the same time, Argentina, which had previously requested to join, later withdrew its request following the election of Milei (who has an ultraliberal and pro-US stance).

In January 2025, Indonesia became a full member of the BRICS. With an expected annual economic growth of 5.1% until 2026, Indonesia represents a significant addition to the bloc, offering new opportunities for economic and commercial expansion. Additionally, between October 22 and 24, 2024, during the sixteenth edition of the BRICS Summit held in Kazan, Russia (Norton, 2024), 13 countries were invited to participate as "partner countries." These countries are: Algeria, Belarus, Bolivia, Cuba, Indonesia (before its official membership), Kazakhstan, Malaysia, Nigeria, Thailand, Turkey, Uganda, Uzbekistan, and Vietnam. This status allows them to engage with BRICS initiatives and benefit from the group's cooperation. With the inclusion of these new members, BRICS Plus now represents approximately 44% of global GDP, as we have mentioned, and holds nearly half of the world's oil reserves (Bhowmick, 2024), consolidating its position as a major international economic bloc and becoming a group essential for global economic growth, particularly for the development of the Global South. During the Kazan Summit, in fact, the interest of many countries from the Global South in joining the group was reiterated, and an endorsement was established regarding the modalities for access to the group (BRICS, 2024). There are also other countries that have expressed interest in applying for membership in the group, such as Venezuela. In this case, as we are writing this book, this accession seems quite complicated due to the opposition of the Brazilian government (Galarraga Gortázar, 2024).

The expansion of BRICS Plus, therefore, reflects the goal of creating an alternative front to the financial and political institutions traditionally dominated by the West, promoting a more balanced and representative global governance for emerging economies. Given the aforementioned limitations, it is worth remembering that this initiative undoubtedly challenges the international system led by the US and, more generally, the West, which has already become obsolete, and instead marks a new and practically necessary phase toward building a multipolar world and, consequently, a new world order.

The G7 and the G20

As we know, the G7, or Group of Seven, represents the group that brings together seven of the world's most advanced economies with the largest GDPs. Until 2014, the G7 was accompanied by the G8, which also included Russia (later suspended due to the events in Crimea in 2014). The group is composed of Canada, France, Germany, Japan, Italy, the United Kingdom, and the US, while the EU participates in the meetings with its own representation as a permanent guest (Laub, 2014). Although it is officially considered that the G7 is composed of this group, which represents the main economic powers by GDP, the reality shows something different: in recent years, the BRICS group has surpassed the GDP of the G7. It is important to emphasize that this group, which today covers a significant part of the world geographically and expanded in 2024, as we mentioned, also represents a considerable share of the global economy and GDP, likely set to surpass that of the G7 in the near future. The latest expansion of the BRICS, in 2025 with the inclusion of Indonesia, the fourth most populous country in the world, along with the inclusion of the previously mentioned partner countries, has led to an increase in the total population of the group, as well as GDP growth and an increase in controlled energy resources, as we have seen.

On the other hand, the countries of the G7, adding up the data from their seven members, recorded an estimated GDP of 46.3 trillion dollars in 2023, representing 26.6% of global GDP and contributing 13.7% to global economic growth over the past 10 years (2013–2023). In 2024, the G7 accounted for 25.4% of global GDP. Additionally, the G7 countries have a population of 780 million people (World Economics, n.d.), which is significantly fewer compared to the other bloc. Within the group, the EU is an "unnumbered member" and, consequently, does not assume the rotating presidency of the G7.

In our view, a growing competition is emerging between the G7 and BRICS blocs, especially between China and the US, while relations with Russia have further cooled after the war in Ukraine and sanctions from G7 members. This alignment dynamic strongly influences the EU's perspective on global governance and its approach to emerging powers.

Regarding the G20, or Group of 20, it was created in 1999 in the context of global economic turbulence, such as the Asian financial crisis. The need to bring together the countries with the largest economies became evident: a platform for dialogue between the major developed and emerging economies was needed to ensure global economic stability. Initially, the meetings were held at the level of finance ministers and central bank governors, but since 2008, with the onset of the global economic crisis, they have been held at the level of heads of state, making the G20 one of the key platforms for addressing global challenges. The group consists of 19 countries and the EU, which participates as a single entity. In addition to the G7 members, the G20 includes a group of emerging economies: Argentina, Australia, Brazil, China, India, Indonesia, Mexico, Russia, Saudi Arabia, South Africa, South Korea, and Turkey. Together, G20 countries represent approximately 85% of global GDP, 75% of global trade, and two-thirds of the global population.

The fundamental principle of the G20 is dialogue on equal terms between the largest global economies, without a rigid hierarchy as exists, for example, in the UN. Participants discuss global issues that transcend national borders, including financial stability, sustainable economic growth, climate change, international trade, poverty reduction, digital transformation, and cybersecurity. The G20 regularly publishes recommendations and collective statements that influence the global economic agenda, although its decisions are not binding but rather advisory in nature.

For Russia, participation in the G20 has strategic importance, as it provides the opportunity to interact directly with the world's major economies and promote its own national interests. Unlike the G7, the G20 format allows Moscow to expand its diplomatic and economic horizon, addressing issues such as energy, regional security, and the construction of a new architecture of global governance that takes into account the interests of all participants, not just Western powers.

The G20 naturally overlaps with the BRICS. Many BRICS countries are also part of the G20, which allows them to harmonize their positions within both forums. BRICS represents a kind of "voice of emerging economies" and promotes a multipolar vision of the world; therefore, they believe that within the G20, greater prominence should be given to countries from the Global South, as well as strengthening cooperation, especially as a result of the increasingly cyclical crises that characterize the current era (Larionova & Shelepov, 2019; Cooper, 2014). Within the G20, BRICS members can influence the global agenda, seeking to balance the interests of the developing world with those of the G7 countries.

The G20 plays a key role in regulating global processes and is an influential platform for dialogue to address issues that affect all of humanity, such as the global economy, ecology, and digitalization. In an increasingly interconnected world, characterized by challenges such as climate change, geopolitical crises, and post-pandemic recovery, the G20 continues to grow in importance, demonstrating that only through multilateral dialogue can compromises be found for collective benefit.

In conclusion, both the BRICS Plus strategy and forums such as the G7 and G20 represent concrete examples of how the world structure is changing, and within it, those countries gaining greater international relevance are leading the Global South to make a multipolar world a reality in practice, thereby contributing to the construction of a new international order.

References

Acharya, A. (2014). *The end of American world order*. Polity.

Acharya, A. (2017). After liberal hegemony: The advent of a multiplex world order. *Ethics & International Affairs, 31*(3), 271–285. https://doi.org/10.1017/S089267941700020X

Andreoni, M. & Casado, L. (2019, November 15). Brics faz dez anos. *Dialogo Chino*.https://dialogochino.net/pt-br/infraestrutura-pt-br/31731-brics-faz-dez-anos/

Bhowmick, S. (2024, December 26). BRICS: una forza per la multipolarità. *ISPI*. https://www.ispionline.it/it/pubblicazione/brics-dopo-le-parole-i-fatti-195250

BRICS. (2024, October 23). XVI BRICS Summit, Kazan Declaration. Link. https://cdn.brics-russia2024.ru/upload/docs/Kazan_Declaration_FINAL.pdf?1729693488349783

BRICS Leaders Meeting. (2017, September 04). The 9th BRICS Summit Xiamen Declaration. http://www.brics.utoronto.ca/docs/170904-xiamen.html

BRICS Leaders Meeting. (2023, August 23). The 15th BRICS Summit: Johannesburg II Declaration. *BRICS and Africa: "Partnership for Mutually Accelerated Growth, Sustainable Development and Inclusive Multilateralism"*, Sandton, Gauteng, South Africa. https://www.gov.za/sites/default/files/speech_docs/Jhb%20II%20Declaration%2024%20August%202023.pdf.

Brolsma, M., de Bruin, R., & Lok, M. (Eds.). (2019). *Eurocentrism in European history and memory*. Amsterdam University Press. https://doi.org/10.2307/j.ctvr7f5v5

Cooper, A. F. (2014). The G20 and contested global governance: BRICS, Middle powers and small states. *Caribbean Journal of International Relations & Diplomacy, 2*(3), 87–109. https://journals.sta.uwi.edu/ojs/index.php/iir/article/view/495

Cossa, R. A., & Brad Glosserman, B. (2022). Regional overview: Washington 'pivots' to Asia. *Comparative Connections, 24*(2), 1–20.

Fukuyama, F. (1992). *The end of history and the last man*. The Free Press.

Galarraga Gortázar, N. (2024, October 25). Brazil blocked Venezuela's entry into BRICS due to post-election betrayal. *ELPAIS International*. https://english.elpais.com/international/2024-10-25/brazil-blocked-venezuelas-entry-into-brics-due-to-post-election-betrayal.html.

Gilpin, R. (1981). *War and change in world politics*. University Press.

Gramsci, A. (2014). *Quaderni del carcere*, Vol. I, Quaderni 1–5, Quaderno 3 (1930). Einaudi, 281–417.

Holzner, M. (2024, August 04). BRICS plus: New world order after the Pax Americana?. *The Vienna Institute for International Economic Studies*. https://wiiw.ac.at/brics-plus-new-world-order-after-the-pax-americana-n-623.html

Ikenberry, J. (2018). Why the liberal world order will survive. *Ethics & International Affairs, 32*(1), 17–29.

Kaufmann, E., & Sielker, F. (2020). The influence of the Belt and Road Initiative in Europe. *Regional Studies, Regional Science, 7*(1), 288–291. https://doi.org/10.1080/21681376.2020.1790411

Krauthammer, C. (2002). The unipolar moment revisited. *The National Interest, 70*, 5–17.

Kupchan, C. A. (2020). *Isolationism: A history of America's efforts to shield itself from the world*. University Press.

Larionova, M., & Shelepov, A. (2019). The G20 and BRICS: Engaging With international institutions for global governance. *South African Journal of International Affairs, 26*(4), 643–661.

Laub, Z. (2014, May 09). The Group of Seven (G7). *Council of Foreign Relations*. https://www.files.ethz.ch/isn/179927/group%20of%20seven.pdf

Mahbubani, K. (2009). *The New Asian Hemisphere. The irresistible shift of global power to the east*. Public Affairs.

Norton, B. (2024, October 26). BRICS grows, inviting 13 new 'partner countries' at historic summit in Kazan, Russia. *Geopolitical Economy*. https://geopoliticaleconomy.com/2024/10/26/brics-13-partner-countries-summit-kazan-russia/.

Petrone, F. (2025). The European Union, the BRICS countries, and the Global South: Rethinking multilateralism and global governance in a time of polycrisis. *International Critical Thought, 15*(3), 419–436. https://doi.org/10.1080/21598282.2025.2554499

Smotrytska, M. (2020, September 01). Belt and Road in the EU, Central and East Europe: Roads of challenges. *Modern Diplomacy*. https://moderndiplomacy.eu/2020/09/01/belt-and-road-in-the-eu-central-and-east-europe-roads-of-challenges/

Stuenkel, O. (2016). *Post-western world: How emerging powers are remaking global order*. Polity Press.

Stuenkel, O. (2023, June 22). BRICS faces a reckoning. *Foreign Policy*. https://foreignpolicy.com/2023/06/22/brics-summit-brazil-russia-india-china-south-africa-putin-nonalignment-global-south/

Waltz, K. (1979). *Theory of international politics*. McGraw-Hill.

World Bank. (2025). China – Data. World Bank. Retrieved July 30, 2025, from https://data.worldbank.org/country/china

World Bank. (n.d.). Data. Retrieved July 30, 2025, from https://data.worldbank.org

World Economics. (n.d.). Retrieved September 30, 2025, from https://www.worldeconomics.com/Regions/G7/

Zakaria, F. (2008). *The Post-American world*. W. W. Norton & Company.

CHAPTER 5

Global South and South–South Cooperation

Abstract This chapter explores the evolving role of the Global South within the international system through the lens of BRICS cooperation and its expanding influence in Latin America and Africa. Beginning with Brazil's 2025 presidency of the BRICS, the analysis situates the group's growing identification with the Global South as both symbolic and strategic. Rather than representing a single hegemonic actor, BRICS embodies a collective aspiration among emerging economies to reshape global governance and promote a multipolar system grounded in equity and inclusivity. The first section revisits the historical and conceptual foundations of the Global South, tracing its evolution from postcolonial solidarity movements such as Bandung and the Non-Aligned Movement to its current rearticulation as a political and epistemic project seeking recognition in global decision-making. The chapter argues that, beyond its geographical and economic connotations, the Global South represents a demand for decolonized governance structures and fairer participation within international institutions long dominated by Western powers. The second section examines the resurgence of South–South Cooperation as an alternative development paradigm, emphasizing how the BRICS—especially through the New Development Bank and the BRICS Plus expansion—have positioned themselves as central actors in this process. The inclusion of new members and the consolidation of intra-South partnerships reflect an emerging global architecture that challenges traditional aid and

F. Petrone, *The BRICS and the Transformation of Global Power*,
https://doi.org/10.1007/978-3-032-23540-4_5

conditionality models historically imposed by Bretton Woods institutions. Subsequently, the analysis focuses on the "Latin American dilemma": whether to remain aligned with the liberal West or to move closer to BRICS' non-interventionist and development-oriented framework. The discussion highlights Brazil's centrality within the group, China's and India's growing presence in regional trade and infrastructure, and the political fatigue of Latin American societies toward Western-led governance. Finally, the chapter examines Africa's role as both a testing ground and a key partner for BRICS' global strategy. While cooperation promises infrastructure investment, technological transfer, and expanded trade, it also raises concerns about new asymmetries within South–South relations. Ultimately, the chapter contends that BRICS' engagement with the Global South reveals both the potential and the contradictions of an emerging post-Western order in global governance.

Keywords BRICS • Global South • South–South Cooperation • Global Governance • Latin America • Africa

Introduction

Beginning on January 1, 2025, Brazil took over the rotating presidency of the BRICS group for one year and set out its agenda with the motto: "*Fortalecendo a Cooperação do Sul Global para uma Governança mais Inclusiva e Sustentável*" (Strengthening Global South Cooperation for More Inclusive and Sustainable Governance). This starting point underscores the significance and priority the BRICS attach to the Global South, to the extent that they dedicated an entire year of their presidency to this focus.

However, it is not only this year that a country holding the presidency has dedicated its leadership to the Global South. For example, in 2023, when South Africa chaired the group, it adopted the motto: "BRICS and Africa: Partnership for mutually accelerated growth, sustainable development, and inclusive multilateralism." Similarly, the Russian presidency in 2024 chose a motto which, although it did not directly mention the Global South or a specific area of the Global South as South Africa did in 2023, nonetheless referred to key themes for the group, such as global development and multilateralism ("Strengthening Multilateralism for Equitable Global Development and Security").

From these few examples, it becomes clear how important the role of the Global South is for BRICS, who have often reiterated their commitment to giving it a voice. Regarding this point, according to various Western analysts, leadership over the Global South could spark challenges among the group's members, some of whom may seek a privileged leadership position compared to the others. Indeed, according to some authors, it appears that both India and China are diplomatically competing to be the true and sole voice of the Global South (Palit, 2023).

In reality, the situation is somewhat different. While these countries undoubtedly aim to strengthen their appeal to the Global South, the latter's attraction is not directed toward any single member, but rather toward the group as a whole. Identifying a single leader within the BRICS would imply replicating hegemonic, Western-style, unipolar models. Instead, countries of the Global South see in the entire group a partner with whom many wish to establish new relationships that are less binding and less rule-based, as is often the case with Western countries. For example, in the past, the well-known austerity measures that international institutions like the IMF imposed when lending funds to countries on the brink of economic collapse—along with all the debt-related consequences these countries incurred with the IMF—were undoubtedly seen by many Global South countries as a trap and a new form of dependence on the so-called good governance[1] that these institutions promote.

In any case, to understand the strategies of cooperation and to attempt an analysis of how the BRICS are positioning themselves with respect to the Global South, we believe it is important first to provide an introduction to what is meant by the Global South. Afterwards, we will delve deeper into the issue, seeking to understand why the Global South

[1] The expression *good governance* refers to a model of efficient and transparent public management, which has been applied, especially in the past, mainly to less developed countries or those in conditions of extreme poverty. Based on the observation of poor governance and the failure of previous aid policies, it proposes two key elements: 1) Efficient public management: overcoming corrupt administrations and local political elites, with the eventual privatization of public services to improve their effectiveness; 2) Economic liberalization: promoting a market economy through the complete liberalization of productive activities and trade. This approach can be imposed in a drastic way, through structural adjustment plans, privatizations, and the delegation of social services to non-governmental organizations (civil society). Alternatively, it can be applied more gradually, as indicated in the G8 Kananaskis document of 2002, as noted by Hermet Guy (2008), where the possibility was raised of concentrating aid on those countries committed to following the principles of good governance and promoting economic growth and poverty reduction.

holds a strategic role and examining how, in the case of Latin America—a region that has historically and geographically been closer to the West—different scenarios may now emerge that could bring the region closer to the BRICS. At the same time, we will analyze the most significant perceptions of the BRICS in Latin America and Africa, as these regions play a key role in the future of the group—both in relation to the BRICS Plus strategy and to the interests of the group as a whole and of individual member states.

What is the Global South?

In general, when referring to the Global South, it usually indicates a group of countries that have historically represented the "periphery," that is, economically less developed countries, generally located in the Southern Hemisphere. Their later development certainly has various causes, but one of the most significant factors is likely the influence of colonial powers that shaped their trajectory (Wallerstein, 1974).

This did not occur with the so-called Global North, a term that generally refers to the wealthier countries, mostly located in the Northern Hemisphere, particularly in North America, Europe, Northern Asia, and Australia. However, if we rely strictly on this definition—that the Global South refers to less developed countries and the Global North to more developed ones, along with their geographic location—several problems arise. For example, Australia is geographically located in the Southern Hemisphere, while countries like China, although considered part of the Global South, today possess economic power that, as we know, has nearly reached the level of a global superpower (World Population Review, 2024). Although, in general terms, some traces of correspondence with reality can be found in this definition, the problem of defining what the Global South is becomes more complex, especially in light of the structural changes in today's global system.

According to some authors, the term "Global South" would even be considered an ideological fabrication that creates misunderstandings (Emton, 2024), as well as a geopolitical cleavage that could reflect a world order essentially based on two blocs: the Global North (i.e., the West), experiencing a crisis in its leadership but which, in reality, has imposed the rules over the past 70 years (after World War II, not to mention the earlier periods of imperialism and colonialism); and, on the other hand, the

Global South, seen as the "rising good" ready to upend international institutions, the global financial system, and global governance in general.

For others, the term represents a concept that, in fact, confuses a clear understanding of the current world order and should be used with caution (Nye, 2023), as it does not fully capture the economic changes and the diversity of policies among the countries it is meant to describe.

Finally, Ikenberry (2024) argues that it would actually be more accurate to speak of "three worlds": the West, the East, and the South of the world, each with a different vision of the world order, and each committed to reshaping the global order according to its own worldview.

In any case, beyond the different readings and interpretations, regarding the origin of the term "Global South," it emerged between the 1970s and 1980s (Ballestrin, 2020), when it was used to refer to the so-called Third World countries that adopted a non-aligned position between the West (considered the First World) and the East (the Second World) during the Cold War. In fact, the term was first used to identify those countries that gathered at the Bandung Conference in 1955 and later created the Non-Aligned Movement in 1961. This movement also rose from the ashes of colonialism, animated by an anti-colonial orientation, and from the outset sought to create a different global order. For these reasons, the concept of the Global South symbolically designates the attempt at cohesion that emerged when former colonies engaged in political decolonization projects and moved toward building a "postcolonial international community" (Grovogui, 2011). At the same time, this term must also be seen as an inheritance of what was previously referred to as the Third World (Sajed, 2020).

Over time, the concept has gradually acquired meanings more in line with contemporary reality and the way the international system has evolved. In fact, as early as the late 1990s, and thus after the fall of the Soviet Union, the Global South came to represent a geographical connotation (which we discussed earlier), symbolically designating the countries of the North as industrialized and advanced, while those geographically located in the southern part of the globe were seen as the less developed part of the world.

However, there are significant inaccuracies within this dichotomy. Considering this division solely based on geographic position creates numerous problems, especially in light of recent transformations. Indeed, countries like China and India—commonly considered members of the Global South—are geographically located in the northern part of the globe. Not to mention that, as mentioned, they have significantly increased their economic weight. As a result, this descriptive criterion also proves to be quite imprecise and confusing.

In other cases, it has been suggested that the Global South could be identified with the United Nations' Group of 77. However, this view is not entirely accurate either, considering that: 1) Today, the group is actually a coalition of 134 countries; 2) These countries are primarily considered developing nations, but the Group of 77 coalition also includes countries like China and several wealthy Gulf States. Therefore, it is not just a matter of developing countries but also of countries that are undergoing a period of full development. Finally, the United Nations itself generally uses the term Global South to refer to developing countries (Rising, 2023).

As we can see, there are several attempts to describe what the Global South represents; however, both because of the very nature of the concept and because global relations are constantly evolving, various nuances arise that make its definition more complex. For this reason, from our point of view, we believe that, in general terms, the Global South can be described as that group of countries that has had little participation in international forums and has often suffered negatively from the effects of the postwar international system, more commonly referred to as the LIO, since this system has primarily reflected the interests of Western countries.

In broader terms, it refers to a multitude of countries that have historically suffered, directly or indirectly, from the consequences of colonialism and imperialism, and that, especially from the second half of the twentieth century onwards, have also experienced the negative effects of globalization and the free market. As we will see, it is also against this type of economic system—which, according to them, benefits the North—that the South is rebelling.

Therefore, rather than a precise concept defined within clearly determined borders, the Global South should be understood as a term indicating a new trend, emerging as a result of centuries of exploitation, which today seeks a greater voice in global affairs, and in particular calls for a reform of the global governance system—both political and financial—so that it can reflect the existence of a multilateralism that already, de facto, exists.

The Global South demands greater protagonism both in international forums and in organizations such as the United Nations and the Bretton Woods institutions, which have served as foundations for the

LIO. Obviously, within this group of countries there is a hierarchy between more powerful states and less powerful ones. And the trend seems to be toward a certain competitiveness among the more powerful countries to assert leadership within the group or, as we have mentioned, the existence of blocs of countries like the BRICS, which embody—or seek to embody—the voice of countries excluded from global decision-making processes. It is no coincidence, in fact, that since their first summit, the BRICS have explicitly claimed the right of the Global South to play a more decisive role in international affairs (BRIC, 2009).

Thus, the term "Global South" fits well today to describe that group of countries that challenge the LIO, which is, in fact, already undergoing transformation, and the mechanisms that characterize it: an obsolete and ossified system of global governance, international institutions (those of Bretton Woods) that still suffer from Western interference, and international forums such as the G7, as well as military organizations like NATO, which from their perspective represent concrete manifestations of the will to maintain Western (under US leadership) hegemony over the rest of the world.

South–South Cooperation

The year 2023 marked a decisive turning point regarding the rise of the Global South (De Carvalho, 2023), which, in reality, had already long shown an inclusive capacity and growth of the bloc (Chaturvedi, 2022), consolidated also—and especially—through the so-called South–South Cooperation, meaning a form of privileged cooperation across various areas (economic, humanitarian, etc.), particularly among countries of the Global South, and without the usual need for approval or intercession by the developed countries of the North/West.

In any case, important events took place in 2023. First of all, it was the year when the BRICS announced the implementation of their BRICS Plus strategy, that is, their expansion to include new members from the Global South in order to give fresh momentum to cooperation (Song Yumin, 2017). And, in fact, starting in 2024, as we have seen, new members joined the group, thereby increasing its control over strategic energy resources such as oil.[2] Additionally, other major oil producers, like

[2] With their association in 2024, the members would control 42% of global oil production and 35% of total oil consumption, not to mention approximately 38% of global gas production and more than 67% of coal production (Griffin, 2024).

Venezuela (Prensa Latina, 2023), are seeking to join the group. This aspect is important because, although some oppose the idea that the BRICS are the spokespersons for the Global South (De Carvalho, 2023), it is undeniable that the group aspires to become just that. Some authors warn that the BRICS could turn into the new colonizers of the Global South (Nayyar, 2016). However, it also seems likely that, for historical reasons, namely, the fact that almost all BRICS countries (except Russia) have suffered the consequences of colonialism and/or imperialism, as well as for reasons of proximity and shared experiences of marginalization in international forums (at least until recently), the Global South could see the BRICS group as its natural representative. To this must be added, as we have seen, that as a result of the BRICS Plus strategy, an increasing number of other countries are seeking to join the group.

The other important event of 2023 was the series of summits held in India under the title *Voices of the Global South*, during which issues related to the problems faced by the Global South were discussed (Government of India, 2023). It is highly likely that these summits were aimed at creating an opportunity for India to position itself as a leader among Global South countries (*Times of India*, 2023). In this case, some analysts argue that this objective by India is already creating friction with China, which also aspires to play this leading role and has, over the past few decades, exponentially increased its economic presence (see also the Belt and Road Initiative) in many countries of the Global South (Amighini, 2024). According to Palit (2023), the rivalry between India and China is clearly evident in the struggle for leadership of the Global South. Both countries are aware that they possess the capacity to represent the Global South in major international forums, especially at a time when much of the Southern world is frustrated by the developed world's inability to help address urgent problems such as climate change, heavy debt burdens, the lack of resources for sustainable development, and deficiencies in economic and social infrastructure for the provision of public goods.

Beyond internal disputes, it remains clear that the current vision and actions of the Global South are not driven by "moralism" (Sarang, 2023)—as was the case in the 1990s, when these countries would denounce the misconduct of Western countries, particularly the US—but are now motivated by pure realism. In fact, it is often pointed out that many of these countries do not follow a well-defined line but rather pursue a kind of active non-alignment or active neutrality, as was the case, for example, during the war in Ukraine. During the conflict, many countries of the Global South did not openly side with the Americans and their European partners but instead condemned the war while maintaining good relations with Russia. In fact, in this case, they managed to prevent the Russian economy from collapsing; on the contrary, they even contributed to the growth of its exports (Comfort, 2024). In this context, the position adopted by some so-called middle powers considered part of the Global South, such as Turkey, is emblematic of how alliances and alignments are increasingly shaped by national interests. Indeed, Turkey refused to implement Western sanctions against Russia, despite being a member of NATO, which allowed it to maintain strong trade relations with Russia while simultaneously preserving its relationships with the West and European countries (Özdemir, 2023).

The BRICS in the Global South and the Dilemma of Latin America

In this section, we aim to discuss the role that, in this new possible scenario—especially the growth and expansion of the BRICS—Latin America may have.

In our view, there are historical, economic, political, and even cultural reasons why Latin America, which demographically represents 8% of the global population, is shaping up as a key region regarding the future consequences of this "clash" between international liberalism, of Western origin, and this new model represented by the "Rest," that is, the non-Western countries. Indeed, as we have observed, true power blocs with diverse characteristics are being formed.

In any case, if we analyze the BRICS, its members display heterogeneous political characteristics: on the one hand, the Chinese and Russian governments show a tendency toward more centralized and controlled forms of governance, while on the other hand, Lula's Brazil exhibits markedly different traits. Just to mention one example, Lula has declared that he wants to strengthen the union with the BRICS, but at the same time, he wants to "dialogue with everyone" (Adler & Long, 2023), in the sense that he defends global multipolarity and multilateralism.

Another aspect to consider is that Western countries, particularly the US and Western European countries, historically the main partners of Latin America, are proving incapable of exerting attractive power over the region from a commercial perspective (Nolte, 2023). More generally, they are losing influence in the face of the entire Global South, further exacerbating the gap that was initially opened by colonialism and later by imperialism at the end of the nineteenth century. This does not even account for the recent tariffs imposed by Trump, as well as the expulsion from the US of many Latin American immigrants, often accused of being criminals, which has undoubtedly had, and will continue to have, a significant impact on relations between the US and Latin America. The exception is Javier Milei's Argentina—toward which the US has recently committed to providing economic assistance in response to the country's ongoing crisis. This support is largely justified by Milei's declared closeness to Trump, as well as by the desire to prevent China from gaining greater influence in the country (Magnier, 2025). In other cases, such as Venezuela, which has a regime hostile to the US, Washington has instead demonstrated—and even threatened—an intention to intervene militarily, also raising concerns about a potential campaign of aggression toward Latin America and the Caribbean as a whole (Ng, 2025; Karlin, 2025).

In our view, these events provide further evidence that the Western liberal system is in crisis, as demonstrated both by its limited capacity to establish strategic partnerships with regions that have so far played marginal roles in the global system, and by protectionist policies, hard-power measures, conditional economic support, and more broadly by economic, political, social, and cultural closures. In this sense, the Global South, and Latin America in particular, may gradually distance themselves from the liberal system led by the West, which, although they had supported it, has provided them with few benefits.

According to many analysts, the contemporary world is experiencing a new phase of "cold war" between the two largest powers, China and the US, being waged in various areas: economic, geopolitical, technological, etc. Furthermore, this cold war is materializing into two new types of political models, which represent a sort of complementarity with each other. On one hand, the US presents itself as the spokesperson for the LIO, built to promote liberal democracy worldwide and to benefit all countries with its inherent tendency toward security, welfare, and progress (Ikenberry, 2020). On the other hand, the autocratic tendencies of emerging powers, especially China and Russia, are often highlighted.

The US strategy, along with that of its main European allies (with which, as we know, relations have recently deteriorated), has, however, faced a reality that has often led to multiple criticisms. In general, the international system established by the US has always included forms of interventionism in the affairs of other states to export democracy, often also with a disproportionate use of force and through ambiguous humanitarian support (Zolo, 2009). Furthermore, in recent years, and especially during times of crisis such as the recent pandemic, the US has opted to provide support only to countries that align with them in the battle against China. This attitude has also been reflected in the global governance institutions we discussed in the relevant chapter. In fact, within these institutions, funds are granted primarily to those who adhere to the so-called good governance they promote, which we have already mentioned. That is, to a whole series of guidelines, seemingly presented as "best practices" to follow in cooperation and development, which in reality represent a complete set of liberal impositions that Global South countries must follow to gain greater participation in the globalized world and, more generally, to receive support (especially financial) from these institutions (Weiss, 2000).

On the other hand, although officially communist, China has also embraced the international liberal system, from which it is reaping significant benefits. Unlike the US, it establishes purely commercial/economic relationships with its partners and prefers a non-intervention approach in the internal politics of states. This same view is shared by the entire BRICS group. In fact, the group adopts a non-intervention stance in the internal affairs of other states, with which, through the NDB, they establish predominantly commercial relations oriented toward a vision that leader Xi Jinping defines as "Global Development,"[3] which is an authentic "mission" in which actions should be taken to promote the development of all countries, especially those in the Global South.In practice, these countries are expanding their influence in parts of the world where Western countries are losing influence or are slow to activate strategic partnerships for establishing positive relations. Furthermore, historically, (they have exercised forms of massive exploitation (especially the Europeans) (Rodney, 1972).

The BRICS, with China at the helm, have become increasingly present in these parts of the world, investing and progressively increasing their influence. Therefore, it seems that the new model these countries are

[3] The Chinese leader used this expression, in the sense we have specified, during the BRICS Summit, under the Chinese presidency, on June 23 and 24, 2022. The title of the speech delivered by Xi Jinping was: "Foster High-quality BRICS Partnership, Usher in a New Era for Global Development."

promoting is proving to be more decisive, in other parts of the world, than the Western model. In addition to the already significant presence of BRICS countries in Africa (Deych, 2015), the case of Latin America is exemplary because this region, due to its language and culture, as well as its geographical position, would be considered part of the West. However, as has been ironically stated, Latin America represents the "far West" (Rouquié, 1989), and thus a kind of marginal appendage of this part of the world. Furthermore, the so-called Monroe Doctrine, dating back to 1823, is famous for essentially establishing the complete submission of the entire American continent to the hegemony of the US.

However, several things are changing today. First of all, for several decades now, Latin American countries have felt like victims of the weight of the Bretton Woods institutions. In fact, in these countries, a famous (among others) theory of international politics was formed, known as "Dependency," which emerged in the 1960s and 1970s. This theory criticizes the fact that in Latin America, the old forms of political and economic dependence were replaced, in the second half of the twentieth century, by a new type of "dependence" on international capitalism, multinational corporations, and, therefore, neoliberal globalization. This theory highlights the negative role and devastating impact of international structural factors, such as the influence of the US, the role of international financial institutions, and the presence of multinational corporations that have strongly conditioned the economy and politics of the region (Kacowicz & Wajner, 2021).

In addition, during the pandemic period, the governments of the US and Europe were often reluctant to come to the aid of these countries. The real help for Latin American countries came from China and Russia. In general, however, in recent years, rivalries have intensified, especially between the US and China, as we know, and unfortunately, these tensions also find a field of confrontation in Latin America, where US policies of closure, and purely anti-China measures, seem to correspond with a progressive increase in the strategic presence of the rival country and its main allies. Precisely in relation to this aspect, it is emblematic that during the pandemic, the US agency USAID—which, it should be noted, has been almost entirely dismantled by the re-elected President Trump (Debusmann, 2025)—cut the budget allocated to the Pan American Health Organization (Kirkpatrick & León Cabrera, 2020). This episode had significant repercussions in the region, particularly in countries like Ecuador and Bolivia, which have fragile healthcare systems and recorded high COVID-19 mortality rates. At the same time, other decisions toward Latin American states by the US had disastrous effects during this emergency period. For example, despite calls from the UN Secretary-General to suspend international sanctions and the embargo imposed by the US on countries like Cuba and Venezuela (as well as other countries in the Global South such as Iran), Washington refused to lift them (Heine, 2021). This situation did not change even during the Biden administration. In fact, for the Democratic president, the competition for supremacy with China was the main objective of US foreign policy, and Latin America has been one of its main battlegrounds.

What is happening in this region opens up several scenarios for Latin American countries, which today find themselves at a crossroads: Should they stay aligned with Western countries or follow new blocs like the BRICS (Petrone, 2023)? Obviously, the debates are very much alive, and the issue is highly delicate. In fact, while the territorial proximity, membership in a liberal governance system, and historical relations (although, as we've seen, not always fruitful) with the US have important aspects, on the other hand, relations with China and potentially with the entire BRICS group, though more recent, are fundamental for the economies of many Latin American countries.

For Latin America as a whole, China is already the main trading partner, as it is for Argentina, Brazil, Chile, Peru, and Uruguay individually. China is the largest investor in the mining sector in Peru and the largest buyer of copper, iron, oil, and soybeans in South America (Heine, 2021).

If we trace the recent developments in relations with the US and European countries on one hand, and the BRICS bloc on the other, we discover that when COVID-19 vaccines were developed in 2021, the debate became increasingly intense. In fact, when the vaccines were produced, the need to supply them to the populations of Latin American governments (as well as those around the world) became a pressing issue. However, in this situation, Latin America found itself facing several problems in accessing the vaccines. "Although they were widely developed in the United States, the United Kingdom, and other Western European countries, access to them by developing countries was limited. This created a gap of inequality between the North and South of the world, which is also evident on many other fronts. The expectation of many Latin American governments was that the region would have access to vaccines produced in the United States. This was why, in February 2021, the President of Mexico, Andrés Manuel López Obrador, with Mexico in a critical situation, close to 200,000 deaths from the pandemic, called President Biden to request his cooperation on this matter. However, on this occasion, the response from the U.S. President was negative. Biden emphasized that only once the entire U.S. population was vaccinated could Washington begin to consider exporting or donating vaccines, despite the fact that the U.S. had thirty million doses of the AstraZeneca vaccine in storage [...]. Just a few weeks later, Biden would accept Mexico's request for vaccines, in exchange for assistance in solving the immigration crisis on the southern border" (Heine, 2021 p. 58).[4] In this situation, Russia, China, and India provided their support to Latin American countries in the field of COVID-19 vaccines: this happened in countries like Mexico, whose president publicly thanked these countries, but also in Brazil with Bolsonaro, who asked India for help in facilitating the sale of 30 million doses of Indian vaccines. Ultimately, the support of these countries to Latin America was decisive (and timely) in confronting the pandemic.

In this context, of course, even more debates arise about the future path that Latin America should follow: "One of the arguments used is that Latin America should minimize its ties with extraregional powers such as China, Russia, and Iran, among others, because they are very different and distant countries. This would make a big difference compared to the region's traditional partners in North America and Western Europe, with whom one could trust, because they would share common values and traditions with Latin America. However, in the region's greatest crisis in the last 120 years, which countries responded? China, with its 'mask diplomacy' first (with $215 million in cooperation for the region in 2020, for a total of thirty countries) and then with its vaccine diplomacy, was, by far, the largest supplier to the region. Chile would not be one of the countries that vaccinated the most people if it weren't for the Chinese vaccines Coronavac and Sinovac, whose delivery was ensured well in advance. Russia, with the Sputnik V vaccine, co-produced in Argentina, among other countries, is not far behind. Meanwhile, India, which produces not only vaccines but also syringes in enormous quantities, continued to demonstrate its status as a pharmaceutical power, at least in early 2021, before being absorbed by the worsening of the virus. In other words, without the

[4] Translation made by us.

so-called 'extraregional powers,' Latin America would find itself in a much deeper crisis than it already faces" (Heine, 2021, p. 61).[5]

It is also important to remember that Brazil, one of the largest emerging powers globally, is already a member of the BRICS, and that other Latin American countries, in light of the recent events mentioned, might be interested in joining the group. For example, Argentina had already requested to join the BRICS to find alternative solutions, especially to the economic crisis it is going through, which institutions like the IMF do not seem capable of supporting. However, the election of the ultraliberal Javier Milei as president led the country to withdraw its request just days before the effective entry. In any case, this expansion process of the group, strongly promoted by its members (particularly by China and Russia, who would certainly benefit more), has highlighted how the BRICS Plus strategy is one of the main and most important points to develop in the coming years.[6]

The BRICS' Growing Presence in Africa

In this scenario, then, while on one hand, Western countries are proving to be incapable of developing solid diplomatic and economic alliances with the Global South, on the other hand, the BRICS offer an alternative to the South of the world, promising a greater voice in international affairs, greater technology transfer (as we will see in the dedicated chapter), more attention and potential trade exchanges, and, in perspective, an expanded group under the BRICS Plus strategic expansion plan, in which more strategies could be shared, including, for example, in relation to climate change. Thus, Latin America could be a test case for this shift and, therefore, inaugurate a new global strategy for the region that, while still betting on its strategy of active non-alignment, would, in fact, find itself closer to the BRICS bloc due to economic, diplomatic, and important issues like climate change. This discourse also applies to Africa, where, in recent years, the competition for BRICS influence has become increasingly evident, with China, India, and Russia among the main actors. China

[5] Translation made by us.

[6] South Africa, which inaugurated its presidency in 2023 with the aforementioned theme "*BRICS and Africa: Partnership for Mutually Accelerated Growth, Sustainable Development and Inclusive Multilateralism*," has declared that BRICS Plus will be one of the central topics to be addressed both during its presidency and in the years to come, as it is an evolving process that will surely involve many other countries.

has established itself as the main trading partner of Africa, with trade volumes exceeding 200 billion dollars in 2019, thanks to major investments in infrastructure linked to the Belt and Road Initiative and financing exceeding 60 billion dollars. India, with trade surpassing 90 billion dollars, holds second place as a key actor in the region. Russia, for its part, has strengthened its economic presence, with a 40% increase in trade with Africa in 2024, focusing on strategic sectors such as pharmaceuticals, energy, and agriculture. Brazil, in addition, has promoted and continues to promote greater partnership in Africa within South–South cooperation. These countries use economic diplomacy that, through loans, investments, and cooperation and development projects, links African nations in a relationship of gratitude and dependency (Petrone, 2024). The objective of Beijing and Moscow is not only economic but also geopolitical: on one hand, they seek access to natural resources to sustain their growth; on the other, they bet on the expansion of export markets in a continent with a rapidly growing population. However, the stakes are even higher, and in practice, as with the interest in Latin America, it is about challenging the influence of the US and Europe in the attempt to build a multipolar world order. Events such as the Russia-Africa Economic and Humanitarian Forum and the initiatives of the Roscongress Foundation (Roscongress, n.d.) attest to the growing Russian activism on the continent, while China continues to consolidate its presence with large-scale investments. This competition for leadership in the Global South, therefore, represents a key element in the redefinition of global balances in the twenty-first century.

How Are the BRICS Perceived Today in Latin America and Africa?

Beyond the aforementioned economic issues, the dynamics that emerged during the pandemic and the recent shifts in the international system raise an important question: How are the BRICS perceived today in Latin America and Africa?

Focusing on Africa first, the group is viewed in a complex and ambivalent way—oscillating between strategic opportunities and structural risks. The 2024 expansion, which brought in new African members such as Egypt and Ethiopia, marks a significant moment for the continent's role in global governance. This inclusion reflects the pragmatic interests of powers like China, India, Brazil, and Russia, which see Africa both as an economic opportunity and as a strategic ally in advancing a more multipolar international order. The accession of new African members opens the door to deeper interstate ties, new financial agreements, and substantial investments, with potential benefits such as reduced regional financial risks (Zelenova, 2024). Many African countries also regard the BRICS as a means to enhance their global influence and, more specifically, as a way to strengthen Africa's voice on the international stage, given the perception of marginalization within the current global order—particularly in the IMF, World Bank, and United Nations. This aspiration reflects the continent's longstanding desire for greater representation in key multilateral institutions where their voice has traditionally been limited.

Yet, concrete economic prospects remain uncertain. Africa faces high levels of indebtedness and significant cuts to development aid: according to the OECD, funding from Western donors is projected to decline by 9–17% in 2025 (The Africa Report, 2025). One might ask whether relief could come from the BRICS, which now account for roughly 44% of global GDP. However, it is legitimate to question whether—behind the rhetoric of South–South solidarity—their approach reproduces dynamics reminiscent of old colonial powers, masking unequal power relations. This asymmetry is especially evident in the dominant role of China, which has been Africa's main trading partner for the past 15 years and represents nearly half of the BRICS' total GDP (The Africa Report, 2025).

Despite these challenges, cooperation between the BRICS and the African Union (AU) could help address some of the continent's historical problems, such as weak internal connectivity, by facilitating access to new technologies and infrastructure that foster regional integration (African Development Bank, 2013). This vision is explicitly endorsed in the Second Johannesburg Declaration, which reaffirms mutual support for the AU's Agenda 2063 and its integration efforts, including through the African Continental Free Trade Area. The declaration emphasizes "the importance of strengthening the partnership between BRICS and Africa to unlock mutually beneficial opportunities for increased trade, investment and infrastructure development," and calls for reducing tariffs and non-tariff barriers on African exports (BRICS, 2023). African delegates actively participate in BRICS events not only for economic gains but also to explore political and developmental alternatives: new trajectories for innovation, climate change solutions, green energy, food sovereignty, and the valorization of indigenous knowledge. However, African influence on BRICS declarations often remains limited by the priorities of the host countries. For instance, the 2020 Russian declaration (BRICS, 2020) focused on historical memory and the fight against Nazism (points 3 and 4), while South Africa's contributions have emphasized Pan-Africanism and climate change. It will be interesting to see which themes the new African members introduce when they host future summits.

The inclusion of more African states (such as Egypt, Ethiopia, and potential members like the Democratic Republic of Congo, Zimbabwe, and Angola) also alters South Africa's position, which may increasingly focus on regional interests. Yet, the presence of three major regional players does not guarantee full continental representation, and Nigeria's stance remains uncertain, as it is currently only a partner member. A structured partnership between the BRICS and the AU could be strategically valuable, but faces institutional complexities and the AU's continued dependence on external funding. Although the BRICS were originally conceived to represent the voices of developing countries—echoing the spirit of the 1955 Bandung Conference—and seek to reform traditional global institutions such as the UN, IMF, and World Bank to ensure greater equity, they have also created alternative instruments like the abovementioned NDB and the CRA to reduce dependence on Western institutions, strengthen intra-group ties, and pursue shared strategic goals. However, as some authors point out (Naidu, 2025), internal tensions, historical rivalries, geopolitical competition, lack of trust, and divergent national priorities may undermine the group's effectiveness. A more critical view, articulated by Patrick Bond (CADTM, n.d.), argues that BRICS–Africa relations risk replicating modern forms of colonial exploitation. According to Bond, the group's policies often perpetuate "unequal ecological exchange," whereby African resources are extracted without fair compensation and under disadvantageous labor conditions. The NDB, he argues, is an "illusion of change," while conflicts of interest and corruption among BRICS and African elites hinder genuine development. In another edited volume (Bond et al., 2019), Bond and other scholars argue that although the BRICS were initially viewed as a promising alternative to Western dominance, they are increasingly perceived as new agents of external interference and resource exploitation in Africa. Across the continent, various forms of resistance have emerged to challenge their expanding influence—from opposition to large-scale infrastructure projects, such as China's Belt and Road Initiative in East Africa, to protests against extractive industries in the Niger Delta. These movements expose the gap between the BRICS' proclaimed solidarity and their actual practices, revealing how local elites often collaborate in perpetuating unequal power relations.

In sum, in Africa the BRICS are perceived as both an opportunity and a risk: they provide tools for global influence, regional integration, and South–South cooperation, yet they also entail power asymmetries, internal tensions, divergent interests, and potential exploitative practices. The ability of African countries to effectively negotiate their participation will be crucial in transforming these opportunities into tangible and sustainable benefits.

In the Latin American context, the BRICS and the recently expanded BRICS Plus framework are perceived with a combination of economic pragmatism and political caution. The region closely monitors the expansion of the group, which from its original core was extended to additional countries at the beginning of 2024 (as we have seen). Despite the absence of Latin American members in this initial enlargement (Argentina withdrew due to Javier Milei's election), several countries in the region, including Bolivia, Cuba, Nicaragua, and Venezuela, have expressed interest in joining, while others, such as Colombia and Mexico, prefer a more pragmatic and gradual approach. Argentina, by contrast, has opted not to participate, reflecting a foreign policy line closer to the US (Glukhov, 2025). Brazil, as a founding member of the BRIC, plays a crucial role in shaping the regional perception of the BRICS. While sharing some concrete objectives of the group—such as reducing dependence on the US dollar and strengthening the NDB—Brazil maintains a balanced foreign policy, avoiding overt alignment with China and Russia. This strategy reflects Brazil's interest in consolidating its role as a global actor in a multipolar world without compromising relations with the West (Konrad-Adenauer-Stiftung, 2023). Nonetheless, it must be said that the US' recent tariff policies toward the country could have a decisive impact on this type of strategy. Conversely, the potential inclusion of countries such as Venezuela—opposed by both Brazil and India, which consider President Nicolás Maduro's mandate beyond January 9, 2025, as illegitimate (ISPI, 2024)—or Nicaragua could reinforce the anti-Western dimension of the group, raising concerns about excessive geopolitical polarization.

From an economic perspective, BRICS Plus is seen as offering tangible opportunities. The NDB provides an alternative to traditional financial institutions, offering less restrictive loans and promoting infrastructure investments. However, based on the active non-alignment perspective we discussed earlier—which, as we described, seemed to waver during the COVID period—effective participation requires autonomous and forward-looking foreign policies. From this perspective, Latin American countries should balance the benefits of access to the group with the need to maintain stable relations with both Washington and Beijing, avoiding becoming instruments of the geopolitical ambitions of the most influential members (Fortin et al., 2021).

Joining or cooperating with BRICS Plus also entails significant political and economic prerequisites. Politically unstable states risk undermining internal cohesion and the effectiveness of joint initiatives, whereas a gradual approach—such as that of "BRICS partner countries"—allows access to economic benefits without assuming full political commitment. In this regard, countries like Brazil and Uruguay pursue coherent, long-term strategies, while others, such as Colombia, adopt more reactive, short-term positions (Glukhov, 2025).

In summary, the perception of the BRICS in Latin America is ambivalent: on one hand, the group represents economic opportunities and a platform for enhancing global influence; on the other, it exposes countries in the region to delicate political and diplomatic challenges. Success in integrating into BRICS Plus will depend on the ability of Latin American governments to combine national autonomy, multilateral engagement, and long-term strategic interests, avoiding subordination to the geopolitical objectives of China and Russia. Moreover, the doctrine of "active non-alignment," prevalent in several diplomatic and academic circles in the region, appears increasingly under strain. The contemporary world seems progressively polarized between a US-led West, which is rediscovering coercive measures and hard power through unilateral actions—such as the already mentioned tariffs imposed under the Trump administration—and an emergent "Rest," ideally led by the BRICS, aiming to reshape the current world order and global governance. In this context, Latin American countries will face the challenge of carefully negotiating their autonomy and strategic space.

References

Adler, D., & Long, G. (2023, January 01). Lula's foreign policy? Encouraging a multipolar world. *The Guardian*. https://www.theguardian.com/commentisfree/2023/jan/01/brazil-lula-foreign-policy-multipolar-world?

African Development Bank. (2013, July 10). Africa and the BRICS: *A Win-Win Partnership?*. https://blogs.afdb.org/fr/afdb-championing-inclusive-growth-across-africa/post/africa-and-the-brics-a-win-win-partnership-12098

Amighini, A. (2024). China's grip on the Global South: Here to stay? *ISPI Policy Paper*. https://www.ispionline.it/en/publication/chinas-grip-on-the-global-south-here-to-stay-169808.

Ballestrin, L. (2020, July 03). The Global South as a political project. *E-International Relations*. https://www.e-ir.info/2020/07/03/the-global-south-as-a-political-project/

Bond, P., Dodd, N., & Van der Merwe, J. (Eds.). (2019). *BRICS and resistance in Africa: Contention, assimilation and co-optation*. Zed Books.

BRIC Leaders Meeting. (2009, January 16). The 1st BRIC Summit; Yekaterinburg Declaration, Russia. http://en.kremlin.ru/supplement/209.

BRICS Leaders Meeting. (2020, November 17). The 12th BRICS Summit: Moscow Declaration, "BRICS Partnership for Global Stability, Shared Security and Innovative Growth". http://www.brics.utoronto.ca/docs/201117-moscow-declaration.html

BRICS Leaders Meeting. (2023, August 23). The 15th BRICS Summit: Johannesburg II Declaration. *BRICS and Africa: "Partnership for Mutually Accelerated Growth, Sustainable Development and Inclusive Multilateralism"*, Sandton, Gauteng, South Africa. https://www.gov.za/sites/default/files/speech_docs/Jhb%20II%20Declaration%2024%20August%202023.pdf

CADTM. (n.d.). BRICS-Africa relations: New strategies to loot Africa. https://www.cadtm.org/BRICS-AFRICA-relations-New-strategies-to-loot-Africa

Chaturvedi, S. (2022). Global South: From myth to reality. *The World Ahead 2023*, ISPI Dossier. https://www.ispionline.it/en/publication/global-south-myth-reality-37079

Comfort, E. (2024, April 01). The Trouble with "the Global South" What the west gets wrong about the rest. *Foreign Affairs*. https://www.foreignaffairs.com/world/trouble-global-south.

De Carvalho, G. (2023). Global South: The "rest" vs the west?. *The World in 2024: The Great Fragmentation*, ISPI Dossier. https://www.ispionline.it/en/publication/global-south-the-rest-vs-the-west-157988

Debusmann D. (2025, October 03). More than 80% of USAID programmes 'officially ending'. *BBC*. https://www.bbc.com/news/articles/cdx2401vn5ro

Deych, T. (2015). BRICS as an Important Actor in Africa. *Insight on Africa, 7*(2), 169–185.

Emton, D. (2024, January 22). Pourquoi le «Sud global» est une imposture idéologique. *Le Point*. https://www.lepoint.fr/monde/pourquoi-le-sud-global-est-une-imposture-ideologique-22-01-2024-2550358_24.php#11

Fortin, C., Heine, J., & Ominami, C. (Eds.). (2021). *El no alineamiento activo y América Latina: Una doctrina para el nuevo siglo*. Editorial Catalonia Ltda.

Glukhov, I. D. (2025). Latin America's integration into BRICS: Challenges and prospects. *Outlines of Global Transformations: Politics, Economics, Law, 17*(5), 82–102. https://doi.org/10.31249/kgt/2024.05.05

Government of India. (2023, November 01). Chair's summary: 2nd Voice of the Global South Summit. https://www.mea.gov.in/bilateraldocuments.htm?dtl/37278/Chairs_summary_2nd_Voice_of_the_Global_South_Summit_November_17_2023
Griffin, R. (2024, February 01). BRICS expansion could see more downstream oil investment. *SP Global*. https://www.spglobal.com/commodityinsights/en/market-insights/latest-news/oil/020124-brics-expansion-could-see-more-downstream-oil-investment-analyst
Grovogui, S. (2011). A revolution nonetheless: The Global South in international relations. *The Global South, 5*(1), 176–190. https://doi.org/10.1353/gbs.2011.0010
Heine, J. (2021). Un orden mundial en crisis. In C. Fortin, J. Heine, & C. Ominami (Eds.), *El no alineamiento activo y América Latina: Una doctrina para el nuevo siglo*. Editorial Catalonia Ltda.
Hermet, G. (2008). *Populismo, democracia y buena gobernanza*. El Viejo Topo.
Ikenberry, G. J. (2020). *A World Safe for Democracy: Liberal Internationalism and the Crises of Global Order*. Yale University Press.
Ikenberry, J. G. (2024). Three worlds: The West, East and South and the competition to shape global order. *International Affairs, 100*(1), 121–138. https://doi.org/10.1093/ia/iiad284
ISPI. (2024, October 21). BRICS: l'America Latina tra dubbi e nuove alleanze. https://www.ispionline.it/it/pubblicazione/brics-lamerica-latina-tra-dubbi-e-nuove-alleanze-187804
Kacowicz, A. M., & Wajner, D. F. (2021). Alternative world orders in an age of globalization: Latin American scenarios and responses. In A. Acharya, M. Deciancio, & D. Tussie (Eds.), *Latin America in global international relations* (pp. 11–30). Routledge.
Karlin, S. (2025, September 08). U.S. attacks on Venezuela are a threat to all of Latin America and the Caribbean. *Left Voice*. https://www.leftvoice.org/u-s-attacks-on-venezuela-are-a-threat-to-all-of-latin-america-and-the-caribbean/.
Kirkpatrick, D. D., & León Cabrera, J. M. (2020, October 27). How Trump and Bolsonaro broke Latin America's COVID-19 defenses. *The New York Times*. https://www.nytimes.com/2020/10/27/world/trump-bolsonaro-coronavirus-latin-america.html.
Konrad-Adenauer-Stiftung. (2023, November 23). BRICS Plus: Latin America. https://www.kas.de/en/single-title/-/content/brics-plus-latin-america.
Magnier, M. (2025, September 26). Trump administration ties Argentina support to rollback of China credit line. *South China Morning Post*. https://www.scmp.com/news/china/article/3326895/trump-administration-ties-argentina-support-rollback-china-credit-line

Naidu, S. (2025, June 26). Engaging the BRICS: A view from the Global South. *FEPS.* https://feps-europe.eu/engaging-the-brics-a-view-from-the-global-south/

Nayyar, D. (2016). BRICS, Developing Countries and Global Governance. *Third World Quarterly, 37*(4), 575–591. https://doi.org/10.1080/01436597.2015.1116365

Ng, J. (2025, September 13). Targeting Venezuela, Trump escalates US campaign of aggression in Latin America. *Truthout.* https://truthout.org/articles/targeting-venezuela-trump-escalates-us-campaign-of-aggression-in-latin-america/

Nolte, D. (2023). The European Union and Latin America: Renewing the partnership after drifting apart. *GIGA Focus Lateinamerika, 2.* Hamburg: German Institute for Global and Area Studies (GIGA) - Leibniz-Institut für Globale und Regionale Studien, Institut für Lateinamerika-Studien. https://doi.org/10.57671/gfla-23022.

Nye, J. S. (2023, November 01). What is the Global South?. *Project Syndicate.* https://www.project-syndicate.org/commentary/global-south-is-a-misleading-term-by-joseph-s-nye-2023-11

Özdemir, A. (2023, February 25). The impact of the Russian War on Türkiye's Foreign Trade. *Insight Turkey, 25*(2), 121–137. https://doi.org/10.25253/99.2023252.8

Palit, A. (2023, September 05). India and China: Close rivals in the G20 and in the Global South. *ISPI Publications.* https://www.ispionline.it/en/publication/india-and-china-close-rivals-in-the-g20-and-in-the-global-south-139661

Petrone, F. (2023). L'america Latina tra due fuochi: con l'Ovest o con "il Resto"? *Il Politico, 259*(2), 36–57. https://doi.org/10.4081/ilpolitico.2023.871

Petrone, F. (2024). The BRICS and Africa, and the train that the EU is missing. *Asian Issues, 1*(9), 75–92.

Prensa Latina. (2023, August 24). Formaliza Venezuela solicitud de ingresar al Brics. https://archivo.prensa-latina.cu/2023/08/04/formaliza-venezuela-solicitud-de-ingresar-al-brics

Rising, D. (2023, September 07). Everyone's talking about the Global South. But what is it?. *AP News.* https://apnews.com/article/what-is-global-south-19fa68cf8c60061e88d69f6f2270d98b

Rodney, W. (1972). *How Europe underdeveloped Africa.* Bogle-L'Ouverture Publications.

Roscongress. (n.d.). Retrieved July 08, 2025, from https://summitafrica.ru/en/

Rouquié, A. (1989). *América Latina: Introducción al Extremo Occidente.* Siglo Veintiuno.

Sajed, A. (2020). *From the third world to the Global South.* E-International Relations.

Sarang S. (2023, August 31). The return of the Global South realism, not moralism, drives a new critique of western power. *Foreign Affairs*. https://www.foreignaffairs.com/world/return-global-south-critique-western-power

Song Yumin, H. E. (2017, September 25). The concept of BRICS plus-a new impetus for South-South Cooperation. *Guardian*. http://tt.china-embassy.gov.cn/eng/sgxw/201709/t20170925_4203086.htm

The Africa Report. (2025, July 05). *What does Africa really stand to gain by joining BRICS?*. https://www.theafricareport.com/387305/what-does-africa-really-stand-to-gain-by-joining-brics/

Times of India. (2023, September 06). G20: How India emerged as the voice of Global South. https://economictimes.indiatimes.com/news/india/g20-how-india-emerged-as-the-voice-of-global-south/articleshow/103410416.cms?from=mdr.

Wallerstein, I. (1974). *The modern world-system I: Capitalist agriculture and the origins of the European world-economy in the sixteenth century*. Academic Press.

Weiss, T. G. (2000). Governance, good governance and global governance: Conceptual and Actual challenges. *Third World Quarterly, 21*(5), 795–814.

World Population Review. (2024). Country rankings. Retrieved September 01, 2025, from https://worldpopulationreview.com/country-rankings/global-north-countries

Zelenova, D. (2024, October 22). African agendas in BRICS: Complications and prospects of Multipolarity. *Valdai Club*. https://valdaiclub.com/a/highlights/african-agendas-in-brics-complications/

Zolo, D. (2009). *Terrorismo umanitario. Dalla guerra del Golfo alla strage di Gaza*. Diabasis.

CHAPTER 6

Climate Change and Sustainable Development

Abstract This chapter examines the evolution of the BRICS' collective role in global climate governance from the 2009 Copenhagen Summit (COP15) to the 2025 COP30 in Belém, Brazil, highlighting the group's growing coordination and influence in multilateral climate diplomacy. Originally conceived as an economic alliance, the BRICS have progressively expanded their agenda to encompass sustainability and environmental governance. Amid the erosion of Western-led climate leadership, particularly following the US withdrawal from the Paris Agreement and the contested credibility of the EU's Green Deal, the BRICS have sought to articulate an alternative vision grounded in multipolarity, equity, and developmental justice. While internal divergences persist—especially regarding energy dependence, economic structures, and policy priorities—the bloc's environmental cooperation has deepened over time. Key milestones include the formation of the BASIC coalition in 2009, the establishment of the BRICS Working Group on Environmental Issues in 2015, and the New Development Bank's financing of green infrastructure and climate adaptation projects. The chapter argues that, despite asymmetries among members, BRICS climate diplomacy has evolved from fragmented responses to a more coordinated stance emphasizing the principles of "Common But Differentiated Responsibilities" and national sovereignty. China's concept of *ecological civilization*, India's advocacy for a "just transition," Brazil's renewed environmental leadership under

F. Petrone, *The BRICS and the Transformation of Global Power*,
https://doi.org/10.1007/978-3-032-23540-4_6

President Lula, Russia's focus on low-emission technologies, and South Africa's Pan-African approach to climate justice collectively reflect diverse pathways toward sustainability. The recent expansion into BRICS Plus—with the inclusion of countries such as Saudi Arabia, Iran, Egypt, Ethiopia, and the United Arab Emirates—adds both complexity and opportunity, reinforcing the bloc's demographic and geopolitical weight while posing new challenges for policy coherence. By engaging in cross-regional cooperation, particularly with Africa, BRICS Plus aspires to promote more inclusive governance mechanisms that challenge the perceived neocolonial tendencies of Western climate initiatives. Furthemore, this chapter contends that the BRICS are transitioning from peripheral participants to central architects of an emerging plural climate order. Their ability to harmonize internal strategies, institutionalize cooperation, and operationalize sustainable development frameworks will determine whether they can transform climate governance into a truly multipolar and equitable enterprise. Ultimately, the chapter provides an overview of how the BRICS group's stance on climate change has evolved from 2009 to 2025.

Keywords BRICS • Climate Governance • Multipolarity • Sustainable Development • Ecological Civilization • Global South

Introduction

The BRICS bloc, often perceived as an unconventional alliance, has recently emerged as a central player in climate diplomacy as well. The group's influence therefore extends beyond economic power, encompassing geopolitical strategies, energy security, and sustainable development initiatives. As the Western-led global order is increasingly challenged, the BRICS seek to offer alternative and cooperative frameworks for climate action (Jinran, 2017), emphasizing multipolar governance, economic inclusion, and technological cooperation.

The collective climate commitments of the BRICS vary significantly. China, for example, has positioned itself as a leader in renewable energy investments and green technology exports, although it remains the world's largest carbon emitter. India, with its ambitious National Action Plan on Climate Change (NAPCC), seeks to balance development needs with sustainability goals. Brazil, despite setbacks during the Bolsonaro administration, has renewed its climate commitments under the leadership of Luiz Inácio Lula da Silva. Russia and South Africa face unique challenges, ranging from reliance on fossil fuels to the need to restructure their economies toward sustainability. The recent inclusion of other countries as partners further diversifies the bloc's energy dynamics, given the dependence of some, like Iran or Saudi Arabia, on oil revenues.

Overall, the group now represents more than half of the world's population and has exponentially increased its contribution to global GDP and international trade. With this demographic and economic capacity, the bloc holds the weight necessary to exert substantial influence in shaping global climate policies, challenging the traditional dominance of Western-led governance structures. Moreover, the recent withdrawal of the US from the 2015 Paris Agreement (White House, 2025), together with doubts about the sincerity of the EU's commitments under its European Green Deal—which several scholars have described as an initiative concealing neo-colonial ambitions (Almeida et al., 2023)—is creating a significant leadership vacuum in global climate governance.

The BRICS group, therefore, is called to play an important role in the fight against climate change and in projects related to sustainable development. However, the economies of the BRICS rely on energy sources that, while supporting their growth, raise significant questions about their ability to adhere to the parameters set in Paris in 2015 during COP21, which established the goal of limiting global warming to less than 2 °C above pre-industrial levels, with an aim to keep it within 1.5°C. Consequently, the group is urged to do its part in addressing this global calamity.

Since their formation, scholars have widely examined the BRICS' impact on global governance and their role in climate-related decision-making. Much of the literature argues that internal differences outweigh common interests, hindering the group's cohesion. Brütsch and Papa (2013), for instance, noted that the BRICS lack sufficiently aligned priorities to shape the international agenda effectively, having failed to reform the global financial system or influence post-Kyoto climate negotiations. The recent enlargement, moreover, is likely to further complicate coordination among increasingly diverse members.

Despite frequent criticism of the BRICS' capacity and political will to confront climate change, their climate diplomacy reveals a more nuanced picture. Most members—except Russia—have long aligned with the G77+China, defending principles such as "Common But Differentiated Responsibilities" (CBDR) and the primacy of national development. In 2009, Brazil, South Africa, India, and China established the BASIC coalition, strengthening their collective voice in climate negotiations and counterbalancing developed countries. At the Copenhagen Summit, they coordinated closely and even considered a joint withdrawal if their stance was ignored—a moment that affirmed their influence as emerging powers in global climate governance. Russia, by contrast, has been only partially aligned with BRICS climate positions. As an Annex I country under the United Nations Framework Convention on Climate Change (UNFCCC), it faces stricter emission commitments and has occasionally supported binding obligations for developing states—a position rarely shared by its partners. Its 2011 proposal for a "periodic review" of countries' economic status, opposed by China and Brazil, further underscored these internal divergences (Martuscelli & Rinaldi, 2016). Such instances reflect Russia's past occasional departure from the broader BRICS consensus, particularly on the responsibilities of developing countries.

Despite early divergences, we observe that BRICS environmental cooperation has progressively deepened, supported by evolving intra-group relations and the regular BRICS Summits, which have strengthened internal cohesion. A key milestone was the establishment of the BRICS Working Group on Environmental Issues in 2015. Its inaugural meeting, held symbolically in Moscow, reaffirmed the group's commitment to the CBDR principle. The declaration states:

> We will consolidate efforts in our respective countries to develop policies and measures contributing to mitigation efforts and adaptation of the national economies to the adverse impacts of climate change in accordance with the principles of equity, common but differentiated responsibilities and respective capabilities, and other provisions of UNFCCC. (BRICS, 2015a)

Another important instrument promoting greater cooperation on sustainable projects has been the creation of the NDB, which can be used to finance green initiatives such as those mentioned in Chap. 1. More broadly, the NDB and the Asian Infrastructure Investment Bank (AIIB) have enabled BRICS countries to invest more than 71 billion dollars in infrastructure and sustainable development projects (Bhowmick, 2024). Just to cite another key example of BRICS climate cooperation, we can refer to the agreement between China and South Africa. In 2018, the two countries signed a memorandum of understanding on climate cooperation, which includes projects on emissions trading, sustainable urbanization, carbon capture technologies, and greenhouse gas management. To strengthen institutional capacity, China also organized online training courses for more than 30 South African officials specializing in climate change (Liquiang, 2023).

Moreover, the BRICS are increasingly aware of the climate challenges that threaten their economic growth and social stability, prompting them to open a dialogue on these issues. This is why the topic of climate change often plays an important role in their summits. In fact, the steps taken by the members have been to institutionalize their collaboration through high-level summits and ministerial meetings in various areas, culminating, as mentioned, first in the creation of the NDB, and later, following President Xi Jinping's proposal at the 13th BRICS Summit in September 2021, China organized the first high-level meeting on climate change in May 2022. During the meeting, the BRICS adopted a joint statement on climate, expressing consensus on accelerating the transition to low-carbon emissions, strengthening the multilateral process, and the need for greater cooperation to address global warming. The joint statement also reaffirmed the role of the UNFCCC and the 2015 Paris Agreement as fundamental legal bases for international cooperation on climate, committing to ensure their full and effective implementation.[1]

The Problem of Climate Change

In general, in the case of climate change, it is essential to reach agreements capable of addressing this urgent calamity. However, on many occasions, especially during the annual Conferences of the Parties (COP), it is difficult to find common answers. The main divergences stem from the fact that industrialized countries in the Global North try to impose binding rules on emissions, while emerging powers, following the principle of CBDR, claim the right to follow a development model that they believe is aligned with that adopted by Western countries throughout the last century (and even earlier). Of course, the recent re-election of Donald Trump as President of the US has further complicated the situation, due to the

[1] More specifically, in the final declaration it is stated that: "Firmly adhere to the principles of the UN Convention and its Paris Agree-ment, including common but differentiated responsibilities and respective capabilities, in light of different national circumstances, and to increase mutual trust, strengthen cooperation, implement the Convention and its Paris Agreement in an accurate, balanced and comprehensive way, in accordance with the institutional arrangement of nationally determined contributions, and based on existing consensus" (BRICS, 2022).

US' withdrawal from the 2015 Paris Agreement (in addition, Trump had already withdrawn the US from the agreement during his previous term).

The current reality is deeply concerning. It is also evident that human activity plays a decisive role in driving climate change and shaping the planet's broader ecosystem. We live in the geological era of the *Anthropocene* (Bruckmeier, 2024), characterized by the profound impact of human activity—from industry and construction to warfare and other large-scale transformations—on the Earth's systems. In other words, our time is deeply shaped by human actions, and addressing these global challenges requires coordinated responses and agreements among governments. Clearly, beyond political divergences, historical, economic, and cultural factors also come into play. In short, aligning such diverse interests around common goals remains a complex challenge.

In any case, since the second half of the twentieth century, the level of destruction caused by global environmental changes has increased alarmingly, leaving an immense impact on all aspects of humanity: the availability and quality of resources, the spread of infectious diseases, dramatic temperature variations, soil infertility and the resulting food shortages, as well as a higher frequency of natural disasters that destroy properties and assets. Ecological issues are influenced by this. Nature is no longer seen as capable of meeting the continuously growing needs. Efforts are being made to invent a new model of economic growth. Nowadays, economic growth and environmental protection are no longer considered mutually exclusive, and the BRICS, like many other economies, have proclaimed the concept of sustainable growth, that is, achieving economic results without causing ecological harm, and even using economic activities to develop ecologically sustainable products and services as one of their priorities. This drastic transition requires substantial structural changes in existing economic models: every economic actor must perceive green growth as necessary and advantageous, encouraging a sustainable economy. This can be achieved through economic support from governments and the legal enforcement of environmental regulations based on in-depth studies related to environmentalism. The urgency of addressing climate change is becoming increasingly evident with the rise of devastating natural disasters and significant changes in global temperatures.

In addition to all this, the impact of the recent COVID-19 pandemic must be considered, as it has profoundly influenced the climate strategies of the BRICS (Tshikovhi et al., 2023), revealing the need for adaptive climate policies capable of withstanding global crises. The pandemic has highlighted the interconnection between public health emergencies and environmental policies, forcing BRICS countries to review their climate strategies and resilience mechanisms. At the same time, what is now defined as the Fourth Industrial Revolution presents both opportunities and challenges for BRICS economies, with digital transformation promising greater efficiency but also exposing the existing disparities between developed and developing countries. Brazil, for example, must face the urgent need to transition to a low-carbon economy, reducing social inequalities and strengthening the most vulnerable populations against the effects of climate change. Russia has adopted a green economy model, seeking a balance between nature conservation and economic progress. However, the COVID-19 crisis and geopolitical tensions, especially the military operation in Ukraine, have underscored the importance of rethinking financial instruments. It is necessary to establish detailed standards, mandatory environmental reporting, and measurable performance indicators for green financing initiatives to ensure sustainable development. In this regard, while Russia's commitment to environmentalism is noteworthy in its public declarations and during the BRICS Summits, it remains insufficient. In fact, according to the Climate Tracker website, Russia's efforts to tackle climate change are very low, resulting in a final rating of "Critically Insufficient" regarding its commitment to climate action (Climate Action Tracker, 2025a). For this reason, further integration of green technologies and financial mechanisms is essential to achieve substantial progress.

The climate policies of the BRICS are deeply intertwined with their socio-economic development goals, making emission reduction strategies highly dependent on economic structures and governance models. International negotiations, such as those within the UNFCCC and COP processes, have become arenas where BRICS countries navigate between their collective and individual interests. However, BRICS countries must constantly strive to reach a common position in global climate negotiations, as cross-border climate cooperation projects and international aid may represent cost-effective solutions for emissions reduction.

Infrastructure plays a crucial role in climate adaptation strategies, especially in Brazil, where road infrastructure is vulnerable to climate risks such as sea-level rise, heat islands, and extreme weather events. Integrating urban strategic planning with climate change adaptation policies is essential to mitigate economic losses. Similarly, China's energy transition remains a key challenge, as the country is the largest energy consumer and the largest greenhouse gas emitter in the world. While China continues with its energy sustainability agenda, ensuring energy security through international cooperation and technological advances is crucial. India's approach to climate governance is characterized by an emphasis on differentiated responsibilities, arguing that developed nations should bear the main burden of emission reductions. India also promotes the distinction between survival emissions and luxury emissions, reinforcing the need for a just transition (CGTN, 2024). As the BRICS countries continue their evolution from participants in climate policies to leaders in global climate governance, their focus remains on strengthening collaboration, promoting technology transfer, and creating inclusive governance structures. The role of the BRICS in post-COP30 and post-COP31 climate governance will be crucial, as these countries push for alternative models that challenge the environmentally dominated policies of the West. Their ability to develop comprehensive roadmaps for emission reduction, improve climate finance initiatives through the NDB, and integrate the private sector and civil society into governance frameworks will determine their success in mitigating climate change while maintaining economic growth. Ultimately, the BRICS nations have the potential to redefine the global environmental governance landscape, but their efforts must be consistently supported by data-driven policy measures and a commitment to multilateral cooperation.

Climate Policies and National Strategies

The BRICS form an alliance whose global impact is shaped by both economic and geopolitical dynamics. Although they share a common identity as emerging powers, internal rivalries and divergent national interests often lead to policy discrepancies. Nevertheless, the group emphasizes collective action on global challenges, particularly climate change. Their growing influence raises crucial questions: Do the BRICS pose a challenge to the existing global order, or do they represent an opportunity to foster a more multipolar and equitable world system? And, if so, could this transition toward multipolarity also generate positive effects on global climate action?

As mentioned earlier, each BRICS nation adopts distinct yet interconnected approaches to climate governance. Below, we summarize the positions and initiatives of the five founding members.

China has shifted from being a reluctant actor to a leader in global climate governance. As the world's largest emitter and leading producer of renewable energy, China faces the challenge of balancing economic growth with sustainability. Its commitment to carbon neutrality by 2060, investments in solar and wind energy, and its role in the Paris Agreement highlight its evolving approach. However, its continued reliance on coal remains a critical issue. China has announced the goal of reaching carbon dioxide emission peaks before 2030 and carbon neutrality, as mentioned, by 2060. As of 2021, the energy consumption intensity per unit of GDP was 26.2% lower than the 2012 levels, and installed renewable energy capacity surpassed one trillion kilowatts. Additionally, according to the 2022 joint statement, a quarter of the global net increase in green cover is attributed to China, which is also actively promoting the development of a national carbon market and providing support to other developing countries for their ecological transition. The country has also pledged not to build new coal power plants abroad (CGTN, 2024).

India adopts a climate diplomacy approach based on equity and historical responsibility, calling for financial assistance for developing countries and implementing national strategies such as the National Action Plan on Climate Change (NAPCC). However, the challenge remains balancing economic growth with environmental sustainability, especially in the energy sector. India has reduced its emission intensity relative to GDP by 24% from 2005 levels, signaling a gradual decoupling of economic growth from emissions. The country has set ambitious climate targets, including achieving 50% of installed electricity capacity from non-fossil sources by 2030, reducing carbon intensity by 45% for the same year, and reaching carbon neutrality by 2070. Furthermore, India's forest cover continues to grow, with 24.62% of its national territory covered by forests and trees. India has also added 23 new wetland sites to the Ramsar list in the past three years, becoming the country with the largest network of Ramsar sites in South Asia (CGTN, 2024).

Historically, **Russia** has played a significant role in climate agreements, from the Kyoto Protocol to the Paris Agreement. However, its current position is heavily influenced by geopolitical considerations and fossil fuel interests. Russia's commitment to carbon neutrality by 2060 is met with skepticism, given its ongoing dependence on oil and gas exports. Currently, 45% of its energy balance already comes from low-emission sources, such as nuclear energy, and the country is developing infrastructure for hydrogen production as a raw material and energy vector (CGTN, 2024).

Brazil has undergone significant political changes under Bolsonaro's administration, characterized by environmental deregulation and increased deforestation. However, under Lula's leadership, Brazil is trying to recover its role as a climate leader, with renewed commitments to sustainable policies and Amazon rainforest conservation. At the same time, Brazil has set a series of targets, including reducing greenhouse gas emissions by 50% by 2030 compared to 2005 levels, achieving climate neutrality by 2050, and eliminating illegal deforestation by 2028. Additionally, it has joined the Global Methane Pledge and established the National Program for Methane Emission Reduction – Zero Methane (CGTN, 2024).

Facing extreme weather events and water scarcity, **South Africa**'s climate strategy is distinguished by a strong normative commitment to equity, most notably through its explicit promotion of a "just transition." Its updated Nationally Determined Contributions (NDC) adopts a "peak–plateau–decline" trajectory, aiming for net-zero emissions by 2050. However, persistent structural challenges—including heavy dependence on coal-fired power and the chronic dysfunction of the state utility Eskom, plagued by load-shedding, corruption, and chronic underinvestment—continue to undermine progress on implementation (Papagiannis, 2025). Particularly noteworthy is South Africa's leadership in advancing a Pan-African approach to climate governance. The country is increasingly positioning itself as a continental champion for climate solidarity, advocating for collective African responses to shared vulnerabilities and development imperatives. Despite its own domestic constraints—ranging from energy insecurity to socio-spatial inequalities rooted in apartheid-era urban planning—South Africa has articulated a vision of African-led climate action grounded in justice, sovereignty, and economic resilience. Through international platforms such as the G20 and initiatives like the Just Energy Transition Partnership, it has amplified the call for equitable, non-debt-creating climate finance arrangements that uphold African agency in decision-making processes (Sidiropoulos, 2024). The 2022 floods in KwaZulu-Natal provided a tragic illustration of how climate risk intersects with historical injustice, reinforcing the urgency of adaptation policies that confront underlying structural inequalities (Time for Africa, 2022). Moreover, South Africa has emphasized the need for greater intra-African cooperation—particularly in expanding renewable energy infrastructure and ensuring sustainable resource governance—underscoring its ambition to forge a unified African climate diplomacy front. This approach aims to both assert African priorities in global forums and leverage the continent's strategic assets, including its abundant solar potential and critical minerals, in support of a just and inclusive green transition (Nair van Ryneveld et al., 2025).

However, despite the good intentions and initiatives mentioned, it should be noted that the five founding BRICS countries are still far from achieving the Paris Agreement goals. In fact, if we consider the Climate Action Tracker website (2025b), the emission targets of the various countries are classified as "Critically Insufficient" for Russia, as previously mentioned, "Highly Insufficient" (China and India), and "Insufficient" (Brazil and South Africa). Their new partners are also classified in these ways. This data indicates that much remains to be done. Likely, the countries have good intentions, evidenced also by various initiatives, but it is necessary to turn those good intentions into concrete actions.

BRICS Plus and Climate Governance

With the expansion of BRICS Plus, which includes countries such as Iran, Egypt, the United Arab Emirates, and Ethiopia starting in 2024, and Indonesia from 2025, the bloc has the potential to amplify its role in global climate debates. However, it will also face greater challenges in creating shared policies and coordination. Moreover, the presence of Saudi Arabia—which, along with Iran, is one of the world's largest oil producers—further complicates the group's credibility in demonstrating a serious and concrete commitment to tackling climate change, although it simultaneously grants the bloc significant leverage in climate negotiations. In the case of Saudi Arabia, the country is implementing "Vision 2030," a strategy to diversify its economy and adopt a circular carbon economy, balancing economic growth with climate concerns (Saudi Vision 2030, n.d.). Nevertheless, its strong dependence on fossil fuels complicates a rapid and effective transition toward a green economy.

However, the internal diversity of the group presents both opportunities and limitations. Although BRICS Plus does not yet have a unified and defined climate policy, its members could play a crucial role as interlocutors for the Global South, promoting more inclusive and balanced climate governance frameworks. The expansion of BRICS to BRICS Plus, which could include additional potential new members beyond the countries mentioned, raises questions about the collective position of the bloc on climate change, but it also presents great potential to influence global climate governance through technology transfer, financial support, and diplomatic coordination, especially toward the Global South. In particular, we believe that greater involvement of the group in Africa, with the recent inclusion of Ethiopia and Egypt, could be a stepping stone in this regard, aiming to elevate the voices of countries that, until recently, had fewer opportunities to be heard, and promoting the transfer of cutting-edge technologies to mitigate climate change on the continent, which is undoubtedly one of the most vulnerable to the issue. This approach had already been highlighted by previous presidencies in South Africa, which had a specific focus on the continent. It is no coincidence that the slogan chosen for the 2023 presidency was "BRICS and Africa: Partnership for Mutually Accelerated Growth, Sustainable Development, and Inclusive Multilateralism,"[2] emphasizing the strategic partnership the BRICS can initiate with the continent in various areas of both growth and sustainable development. This regional commitment, therefore, could be truly crucial in improving climate resilience in vulnerable areas, enhancing infrastructures, and mitigating the socio-economic impacts of environmental degradation. At the same time, greater engagement with Africa potentially represents a critical counterbalance to the Western agenda on climate change and a valid new partner for Africa in addressing the devastating impact that climate change continues to inflict on the most fragile African countries. In fact, Africa remains the most vulnerable region to climate change, despite its minimal contribution to greenhouse gas emissions.

What could position the BRICS as a key interlocutor for Africa is also a widespread perception across the continent that Western countries are not fully committed to addressing climate change. Indeed, the way Western countries are perceived in terms of their climate commitments—and, more broadly, the seriousness with which climate change is addressed in Africa—was highlighted in September 2023, when Kenya hosted the Africa Climate Summit. In the preparations for the summit, more than 400 African civil society organizations wrote a letter to African heads of state, urging them to be cautious regarding the West. According to the authors of the letter, the West had diverted the climate change agenda by pursuing a hidden

[2] During previous summits chaired by South Africa, the slogans were as follows. In 2013 (5th BRICS Summit in Durban): "BRICS and Africa: Partnership for Development, Integration and Industrialisation"; in 2018 (10th BRICS Summit in Johannesburg): "BRICS in Africa: Collaboration for Inclusive Growth and Shared Prosperity in the 4th Industrial Revolution." This highlights both a strategic concern by South Africa, which clearly positions itself as a bridge to Africa, and a genuine interest in more inclusively involving the continent's voice in the global agenda.

agenda harmful to African interests (Chime, 2023). This letter highlights the mistrust with which the Global North is viewed by the Global South. Much of the scientific work supporting the climate change discourse comes from the West. Precisely for this reason, BRICS Plus, when addressing the issue of climate change, will have a greater ability to attract the consensus of those in the Global South who are skeptical of a "hidden agenda" from the West (Solomon, 2024).

Moreover, regarding Western countries, or more broadly the Global North, there are additional factors that worsen their image and influence how they are perceived in the Global South. We have already mentioned the US withdrawal from the Paris Agreement, which in itself reflects a near-complete disinterest by the US in combating climate change. As for the EU and the aforementioned European Green Deal, many criticisms target specific mechanisms, such as the Carbon Border Adjustment Mechanism, which penalizes exports from emerging economies, increasing competition among developing nations for access to European markets and thereby weakening their ability to form a cohesive bloc in climate negotiations (Byiers & Medinilla, 2024). Furthermore, Western countries are often criticized for the financial conditionalities attached to their green transition funds, which are frequently allocated in ways that favor certain countries over others, creating internal tensions within the Global South. The Green Climate Fund, for instance, has been criticized for distributing resources unevenly, prioritizing nations more closely aligned with Western policies (Birger Skjærseth et al., 2013).

BRICS Expansion and Its Implications for Global Climate Governance

The expansion of BRICS, therefore, has the potential to redefine the global landscape of climate governance. According to the Institute for Security Studies (Naidoo, 2023), an independent think tank based in Pretoria, BRICS could be the catalyst for a new global alliance capable of addressing the climate crisis more effectively. The group, which represents half of the world's population and nearly 30% of the planet's total land area, is particularly vulnerable to the impacts of global warming.

A study published by the World Bank in 2018 (World Bank, 2018) predicts that ongoing climate change will cause adverse events affecting approximately 143 million people in the Global South by 2050, leading to various forms of migration and climate mobility, especially in three regions: Sub-Saharan Africa, South Asia, and Latin America. However, the demands of developing countries have long been ignored in global climate negotiations. The expansion of BRICS grants the group greater weight on the international stage, increasing its capacity to influence the global climate agenda and propose solutions that better reflect the needs of emerging economies.

Statements from the BRICS themselves indicate a tendency to address the climate crisis through an inclusive and holistic approach. For example, the Observer Research Foundation, an independent think tank based in Delhi, has emphasized that an expanded BRICS group is better equipped to collectively address global challenges, including climate change (D'Souza, 2021). Despite the lack of mutual trust among many countries in jointly managing the global climate crisis, the group has assumed a leadership role in the multilateral climate process. Sun Zhen, a senior official from China's Ministry of Ecology and Environment, highlighted in an interview with *China Daily* that global warming represents "a common challenge for all of humanity" and that the climate crisis requires countries around the world to unite to confront it together (Liquiang, 2023).

In this context, the BRICS nations have always shown a strong commitment to the common future of humanity. They have not only responded proactively to climate change, but have also actively participated in the multilateral process of global climate governance.

BRICS Plus: Challenges and Opportunities for BRICS Leadership

The 16th BRICS Summit, held in Kazan, Russia, from October 22 to 24, 2024, solidified this developing reality and opened up a significant opportunity for BRICS nations to tackle global challenges, including climate change. The event marked the first meeting after the group's expansion to include Egypt, Ethiopia, Iran, and the United Arab Emirates, joining the original core formed by Brazil, Russia, India, China, and South Africa.

Despite the growing influence of BRICS, various challenges hinder their ability to effectively lead global climate governance:

- **Differences in internal policies**: Differences in political systems, economic structures, and foreign policy priorities complicate coordinated climate action.
- **Dependence on fossil fuels**: Russia, India, China, and South Africa remain heavily dependent on fossil fuels, which undermines their credibility as climate leaders. At the same time, the new members joining the group under the BRICS Plus strategy are major oil producers whose economies are largely based on fossil fuels. These factors further complicate the possibility of a decisive and unified shift in addressing climate change.
- **Technological and financial limitations**: While China is at the forefront of green technology, other BRICS countries face significant limitations in advancing the energy transition. Due to a lack of technological capacity, financial resources, and access to necessary tools, some countries—including several of the new members—encounter greater difficulties in pursuing a green energy transition.

Nonetheless, the BRICS possess significant potential for leadership in global climate diplomacy. The group is increasingly seeking to adopt a holistic approach to climate action—one that integrates diverse perspectives from the Global South and underscores the importance of inclusive dialogue in addressing global challenges. Despite their internal differences, BRICS countries share a vision that diverges from traditional Western models of governance.

For example, China's concept of "ecological civilization," which is present in Chinese political thought, offers an alternative framework that integrates environmental sustainability with cultural and moral imperatives (Martinez, 2024). The idea of ecological civilization proposed by China has resonated widely within BRICS, especially when it came to establishing a common position on sustainability and combating climate change. The growing importance of these issues in multilateral discussions has led BRICS to reconsider global governance mechanisms, attempting to include new narratives that not only address environmental challenges but also promote greater equity in global decision-making processes. In promoting these concepts, China has emphasized the need for a new vision that challenges the current international order and leads to greater representation of developing countries.

As climate change continues to reshape global politics, BRICS nations are increasingly positioned to influence climate governance. Despite internal divergences and limitations, their capacity to steer global climate negotiations, challenge Western-led institutions, and promote a multipolar world order remains significant. While internal obstacles persist, their engagement signals a move toward a more inclusive and potentially transformative global environmental framework. The urgency of climate mitigation and adaptation is undeniable; yet, global responses remain fragmented, particularly in the West, where inconsistent policies and competing economic priorities hinder collective action. This gap creates space for emerging actors, such as the BRICS, to influence climate governance. In this sense, their growing commitment to climate action highlights the group's potential to play a transformative role in global climate governance. The expansion of the group and the deepening climate cooperation among its members signal BRICS' evolution from a primarily economic forum to a key actor in global climate governance. With growing interest from other countries in joining, the group has the potential to reshape the architecture of climate governance, promoting a more inclusive and multipolar order. The bloc stands at a critical juncture: by strengthening internal cooperation, advancing sustainability, and engaging in effective climate diplomacy, it could help build a more multipolar and environmentally resilient future. Yet the members largely remain reliant on traditional energy sources, and the key challenge continues to be the group's ability to present a unified stance in global negotiations.

The Evolution of the BRICS' Role in the Conferences of the Parties from 2009 to 2025: An Overview of Key Points and Positions

COP15 – Copenhagen, 2009

The Copenhagen Climate Conference (COP15) marked a pivotal yet controversial moment in global climate governance. Convened to establish a post-Kyoto framework, it ultimately failed to deliver a legally binding treaty. Instead, it produced the *Copenhagen Accord*, a political, non-binding agreement that recognized the need to limit global warming to below 2°C, introduced the concept of voluntary national pledges, and launched commitments for climate finance, including the creation of the Green Climate Fund (UNFCCC, 2010).

A key development during COP15 was the emergence of the above-mentioned BASIC group—Brazil, South Africa, India, and China—which coordinated their negotiating positions as major emerging economies. Although Russia shared similar concerns as part of the broader BRICS, it played a less prominent role in the negotiations. The BASIC coalition became a decisive actor in shaping the final outcome, negotiating directly with the US and EU. They emphasized the principle of "Common But Differentiated Responsibilities and Respective Capabilities" (CBDR-RC), insisting that developed countries bear the primary responsibility for emissions reductions and must provide finance and technology transfer to developing nations. Furthermore, the group rejected binding obligations for emerging economies, arguing for their right to development and promoting the notion of climate justice—that climate action should not undermine poverty alleviation and economic growth.

Instead of adopting binding emission reduction targets under a common international regime, the BASIC group chose to submit voluntary mitigation pledges, known as Nationally Appropriate Mitigation Actions (NAMAs), within the framework of the UNFCCC (Linnér & Pahuja, 2012). These pledges emerged from the broader debate on how to share mitigation efforts among countries, balancing the principles of equity, responsibility, and development needs.

In this context, each country defined its own voluntary objectives. China pledged to reduce the carbon intensity of its GDP by 40 to 45% compared to 2005 levels by 2020, while India announced a similar goal, aiming to cut its emissions intensity by 20 to 25% over the same period. Brazil committed to lowering its projected emissions by 36 to 39% compared to a business-as-usual scenario by 2020. South Africa, for its part, pledged a 34% reduction below business-as-usual levels by 2020 and 42% by 2025, though these targets were explicitly conditional on receiving adequate international financial and technological support. Russia stated that it would reduce between 10 and 25% compared to the 1990s. However Russia, being an Annex I country under the Kyoto Protocol, followed a different approach, maintaining legally binding commitments rather than submitting NAMAs (Martuscelli & Rinaldi, 2016).

Although the Copenhagen Accord lacked legal force, it institutionalized voluntary contributions and recognized differentiated responsibilities, laying the groundwork for the Paris Agreement (2015). The BASIC coordination demonstrated the growing influence of the Global South in climate diplomacy, asserting a more plural and equitable vision of global climate governance—even as internal differences and the non-binding nature of their commitments limited the bloc's collective impact.

COP16 – Cancún, 2010

At the 2010 Cancún climate talks (COP16), the outcomes of the Copenhagen Summit were formalized into UN decisions, establishing key mechanisms such as the Adaptation Framework, the Technology Mechanism, and the Green Climate Fund (UNFCCC, n.d.-a, n.d.-b). The BASIC countries coordinated their positions to restore trust after Copenhagen and facilitate the *Cancún Agreements*. Their collaborative approach enabled progress on mitigation pledges, adaptation frameworks, and climate finance, moving beyond the rigid "binding or nothing" approach that had previously hindered negotiations. The broader BRICS grouping, including Russia, also influenced discussions, with Russia participating more selectively but reinforcing the position of emerging economies in advocating for equity, differentiated responsibilities, and financial and technological support from developed countries. The BASIC countries emphasized that voluntary national mitigation actions by developing nations should be linked to transparency, reporting, and verification mechanisms, but only if supported by adequate international finance and technology. They upheld the principle of CBDR, ensuring that developed countries assumed binding commitments while emerging economies retained flexibility. India, in particular, acted as a bridge between developed and emerging countries, promoting equitable access to sustainable development and non-intrusive international review of mitigation actions, while advocating accountability for developed nations (Qi, 2011).

Despite some internal divergences on priorities and the degree of acceptable commitments, the BASIC and broader BRICS countries helped produce a balanced Cancún outcome. The agreement incorporated explicit commitments from developed countries alongside voluntary, nationally determined actions from developing countries, with mechanisms for transparency, review, and support. Their engagement highlighted the growing structural influence of emerging economies in shaping international climate governance while safeguarding their developmental space.

COP17 – Durban, 2011

During COP17 in Durban, the *Durban Platform for Enhanced Action* was launched, marking a significant political breakthrough in international climate negotiations. The platform was tasked with developing the foundational elements of a new, universal legal instrument applicable to all Parties of the UNFCCC, addressing the limitations of the Kyoto Protocol. This negotiating process was designed to culminate at COP21 in Paris, ultimately resulting in a more inclusive global agreement (Amorim et al., 2015).

The BRICS countries played an important role in these negotiations. However, the primary influence was still exerted by the BASIC group, which maintained a unified position in favor of equity and the CBDR. South Africa's role as the host country further amplified the group's visibility and strengthened its capacity to shape discussions on climate finance and the implementation of agreed measures, including the operationalization of the Green Climate Fund (Chevallier, 2011).

At the same time, Russia, alongside Japan and Canada, had already announced that it would not participate in a second commitment period under the Kyoto Protocol, arguing that the framework was inherently unbalanced as it imposed obligations only on developed countries. This divergence highlighted the necessity of a truly universal agreement, one that would engage all major emitters in a fair and inclusive framework (Center for Climate and Energy Solutions, 2011). The Durban Platform laid the groundwork for such an agreement, creating the negotiating architecture that eventually led to the Paris Agreement in 2015. Through this process, the BASIC countries helped to bridge the gap between developed and developing nations, reinforcing a model of climate governance based on equity, differentiation, and shared responsibility.

COP18 – Doha, 2012

At COP18 in Doha, the conference produced the *Doha Climate Gateway*, including a second commitment period for the Kyoto Protocol and the launch of the Durban Platform toward a universal climate agreement by 2020 (Center for Climate and Energy Solutions, 2012). Developed countries reiterated their pledge to provide $100 billion annually in climate finance to developing nations, while discussions on loss and damage mechanisms remained limited.

The BRICS countries, acting through the BASIC group with China speaking on behalf of all members, emphasized CBDR-RC, pressed for enhanced financial support, and resisted new conditionalities on climate finance. Their interventions reflected a strong focus on development priorities, adaptation, and mitigation needs, ensuring that the concerns of major emerging economies were central to the negotiations. Although not formal leaders, the BRICS shaped the Doha agenda by presenting a coordinated stance on equity, finance, and development, demonstrating their growing influence in global climate governance and their ability to align national interests with collective advocacy for the Global South (Omuko-Jung, 2014).

COP19 – Warsaw, 2013

At COP19 in Warsaw (November 2013), the climate negotiations advanced the pre-Paris process through guidance on loss and damage and the REDD+ framework (which means: "Reducing emissions from deforestation and forest degradation, plus the role of conservation, sustainable management of forests and enhancement of forest carbon stocks"). Key outcomes included the establishment of the *Warsaw International Mechanism for Loss and Damage* and the *Warsaw Framework for REDD+*, which provided clearer guidance on adaptation, mitigation, and forest-related climate actions. These steps helped maintain momentum toward a comprehensive climate agreement, ultimately concluded in Paris in 2015 (UNFCCC, 2013).

The BRICS countries coordinated their positions, issuing a joint statement prior to the conference, which represented an initial form of collective coordination (Republic of Moldova, 2013). They pledged to strengthen cooperation on climate change, support a comprehensive and balanced Warsaw outcome, and ensure that pre-Paris work programs addressed developing-country needs. In particular, the BRICS emphasized that the *Durban Platform for Enhanced Action* should consider all its pillars—mitigation, adaptation, finance, capacity-building, technology transfer, and transparency—rather than focusing solely on mitigation.

Through these interventions, the BRICS reaffirmed their commitment to the principles of the UNFCCC, particularly the principle of CBDR-RC. While not assuming a formal leadership role, they exerted influence by advocating for equitable treatment of developing countries, promoting financial and technological support, and ensuring that development priorities were integrated into the international climate agenda.

COP20 – Lima, 2014

At COP20 in Lima, the negotiations produced the *Lima Call for Climate Action*, a key procedural step toward the 2015 Paris Agreement. The conference provided the technical roadmap for countries to submit their Intended Nationally Determined Contributions (INDCs), which would become the cornerstone of the future climate regime. Although the outcome was largely procedural, it established the framework for nationally driven commitments and launched the *Lima to Paris Action Agenda* to sustain momentum in the lead-up to Paris (Jacobs, 2014).

The BRICS countries played a coordinated role at COP20 in Lima, emphasizing that the forthcoming Paris framework should uphold equity and the CBDR-RC. In line with the outcomes of the meeting (UNFCCC, 2014), they advocated for a balanced approach that integrated adaptation, finance, capacity-building, and technology transfer into the INDCs, opposing a mitigation-only focus, and called for predictable and scaled-up financial support through mechanisms such as the Green Climate Fund (Amorim et al., 2015). Through these coordinated efforts, the BRICS ensured that the developmental needs and capacities of emerging economies were reflected in the negotiations, reinforcing their influence within global climate governance and paving the way for a more inclusive and equitable Paris Agreement.

COP21- Paris, 2015

In the months preceding COP21 in Paris (2015), the BRICS countries intensified their climate diplomacy and introduced substantial mechanisms for environmental cooperation, moving beyond mere declarations. In April, the inaugural BRICS Environment Ministers' Meeting convened in Moscow, endorsing the establishment of an international platform for sharing environmentally sound technologies to bolster public–private collaboration among BRICS nations (BRICS, 2015a). Subsequently, in July, BRICS leaders met for their seventh summit, emphasizing their readiness to address climate change both globally and domestically and pledging to promote a comprehensive, effective, and equitable UNFCCC agreement (BRICS, 2015b).

At COP21, the BRICS countries played an active and coordinated role, highlighting the importance of upholding the principle of CBDR-RC. They advocated for the integration of adaptation, finance, capacity-building, and technology transfer within the framework of the NDCs, while urging developed countries to fulfill their pledge to provide US$100 billion annually to support climate action in developing nations. Russia, in particular, expressed its commitment to support developing countries through UN mechanisms and actively promoted the creation of a new international climate agreement to succeed the Kyoto Protocol. The BRICS' statements and commitments during Paris underscored their collective intent to shape a fair, inclusive, and effective climate regime, bridging traditional North–South divisions and ensuring that emerging economies' development priorities were reflected.

Through these coordinated efforts, the BRICS contributed significantly to the adoption of the Paris Agreement, helping establish governance mechanisms for tracking NDCs and promoting a model in which both mitigation and adaptation are supported by financial and technological assistance. Their engagement reinforced their role as key actors in global climate governance, paving the way for continued multilateral cooperation and strengthening their collaborative efforts, particularly in aligning increasingly coordinated positions on climate issues. Regarding Russia, its gradual convergence toward more common positions on climate policy is likely driven by a desire to play a more prominent role on the global stage—an ambition that would be difficult to achieve without maintaining strong relations with China and India (Shen & Zou, 2024).

COP22 – Marrakech, 2016

At COP22 in Marrakech, the first conference following the entry into force of the Paris Agreement, the BRICS countries played a key role as major developing nations in advancing its implementation. Their efforts focused on climate finance, technology transfer, and capacity building for developing countries, all crucial for achieving national emission reduction targets. Amid political uncertainty following the 2016 US presidential election, the BRICS reaffirmed their commitment to the Agreement, stressing the need to translate national pledges into concrete actions and to establish clear operational rules ensuring transparency and accountability in global climate governance.

The BRICS were instrumental in supporting the *Marrakech Action Proclamation*, which reaffirmed global political will for climate action, and in promoting the Marrakech Partnership for Global Climate Action, a platform engaging non-state actors. They also emphasized that the Paris Rulebook should reflect differing national circumstances and ensure adequate climate finance for developing countries. Through these contributions, the BRICS helped sustain international momentum for the Paris Agreement, highlighting their strategic role in shaping global climate governance (Fan, 2021).

COP23 – Bonn, Fiji Chair, 2017

During COP23 in Bonn, presided over by the Fiji Islands, the BRICS countries' statements and actions reflected a shared commitment to implementing the Paris Agreement and promoting climate justice. Collectively, they endorsed the *Fiji Momentum for Implementation*, a key outcome of COP23 outlining steps for operationalizing the Agreement in 2018, and supported the launch of the *Talanoa Dialogue*, aimed at helping countries enhance and implement their NDCs by 2020. Individually, BRICS nations reaffirmed their commitment to the Paris Agreement, highlighting the need for clear rules to make pledges transparent and enforceable.

A key aspect of the BRICS position was a strong focus on the principle of CBDR-RC, acknowledging differing national circumstances and capacities. These countries stressed that developed nations must fulfill their climate finance obligations to support developing countries' transitions to low-carbon economies. Additionally, the BRICS promoted sustainable development models that integrate economic growth with environmental protection, encouraged South–South cooperation, and supported the active involvement of non-state actors in climate action. Their participation was crucial in maintaining international momentum for the Paris Agreement (BRICS Policy Center, 2017).

COP24 – Katowice, 2018

At COP24 in Katowice in December 2018, the BRICS reaffirmed their commitment to the Paris Agreement and the 2030 Agenda for Sustainable Development, emphasizing that climate action must align with social justice and support the Global South.

Building on the Johannesburg Declaration (July 2018), BRICS backed the adoption of the *Katowice Rulebook* to operationalize the Paris Agreement but stressed flexibility in transparency and reporting to reflect countries' differing capacities. They highlighted the key role of developed nations in providing finance, technology, and capacity building to enable effective participation by developing countries (International Institute for Sustainable Development, 2018). The bloc also prioritized sustainable energy transition, green financing, and infrastructure development, particularly in Africa, while linking climate action to broader goals such as circular economy, sustainable ocean and resource management, and biodiversity conservation. Overall, BRICS presented climate action as part of a strategy for inclusive, equitable, and sustainable global development.

COP25 – Madrid, Chile Chair, 2019

At the 25th Conference of the Parties (COP25) held in Madrid in 2019, the BRICS presented a unified stance emphasizing the importance of advancing the implementation of the Paris Agreement in the post-2020 period. In their joint ministerial statements, the BASIC countries highlighted the need to conclude negotiations on Article 6, which governs market and non-market mechanisms for international cooperation, ensuring environmental integrity, equity, and a fair transition from the Clean Development Mechanism. They stressed that these mechanisms should allocate a portion of proceeds to the Adaptation Fund and send a strong signal to the private sector regarding its role in achieving global climate objectives (Ministry of Environment and Forests, Government of India, 2019).

The ministers reaffirmed that progress on pre-2020 climate action would serve as a key benchmark for the success of COP25. They called for a biennial work program under the subsidiary bodies to assess gaps and progress, urging developed countries to meet their commitments regarding climate finance, technology transfer, and capacity-building support for developing nations. BASIC emphasized the holistic and faithful interpretation of the Paris Agreement, underlining the urgent need to correct current imbalances in negotiations to enable developing countries to contribute effectively to collective climate action.

Despite the limited progress of COP25, particularly regarding ambition and high-level commitments, the BRICS countries underscored the necessity of increasing climate finance accessibility, supporting developing nations in addressing loss and damage, and strengthening multilateral cooperation. The establishment of the *Santiago Network* was welcomed as a step toward providing technical assistance to vulnerable countries, although the ministers expressed disappointment at the insufficient ambition displayed by major economies.

Overall, the BRICS (and BASIC) position at COP25 reflected their dual focus on ensuring fairness and equity in climate governance while advocating for stronger support and resources for developing countries. The bloc leveraged its geopolitical and economic influence to promote a multilateral approach, calling on the international community to fulfill commitments and uphold the integrity and effectiveness of the global climate regime (BRICS Policy Center, 2022).

Intersessional Online Meetings 2020 (Due to COVID – 19 Pandemic)

During 2020, the regular UNFCCC meeting cycle was disrupted by the COVID-19 pandemic. Online sessions in June and November 2020 allowed updates from constituted bodies and mandated events, while the December 2020 Climate Ambition Summit provided a platform for countries to announce new NDCs and net-zero pledges. In June, the subsidiary bodies held informal online consultations, but no formal decisions were made, reflecting ongoing concerns about inclusivity in the virtual format (Earth Negotiations Bulletin, 2022). During this period, as stated in the Moscow Declaration (points 82 and 83), the BRICS countries reaffirmed their commitment to the implementation of the Paris Agreement, grounded in the principles of the UNFCCC, particularly the principle of CBDR-RC. They urged developed countries to increase financial, technical, and technological support to developing nations to enhance mitigation and adaptation efforts. The BRICS also emphasized environmental cooperation through joint initiatives such as the BRICS Environmentally Sound Technology Platform and the Clean Rivers Programme. Furthermore, they expressed support for the adoption of the Post-2020 *Global Biodiversity Framework*, advocating for a balanced approach that integrates biodiversity conservation, sustainable use, and equitable benefit-sharing (BRICS, 2020).

COP26 – Glasgow, 2021

During the 2021 COP26 Conference in Glasgow, the BRICS countries reaffirmed their commitment to climate action and emphasized the need for an equitable and multilateral approach. While recognizing their shared responsibility to reduce global emissions, the group reiterated the principle of CBDR, stressing that developed countries must provide financial, technological, and institutional support to developing nations to achieve the goals of the Paris Agreement (Chapungu et al., 2022). Furthermore, the BRICS, together with other developing countries, shared the call for industrialized nations to fulfill their pledge to mobilize 100 billion US dollars annually and advocated for reforming multilateral financial institutions to ensure more accessible and timely funding for the Global South (Chatham House, 2021).

Despite a common stance on issues such as climate finance and adaptation, the BRICS countries displayed significant differences in their national commitments. Indeed, India—through Prime Minister Narendra Modi—announced an ambitious plan known as *Panchamrit*, which includes five key targets: increasing non-fossil energy capacity to 500 GW by 2030; meeting 50% of energy demand from renewable sources; reducing total projected emissions by one billion tons; lowering the emissions intensity of GDP by 45%; and achieving carbon neutrality by 2070. Modi also introduced the concept of *LIFE* (Lifestyle For Environment), a global movement promoting sustainable lifestyles. China, for its part, reaffirmed its pledge to peak emissions before 2030 and reach carbon neutrality by 2060, updating its NDCs. These commitments reflect a pragmatic approach that takes into account the distinct economic and social conditions of each country (Ministry of External Affairs, Government of India, 2021).

Overall, the BRICS position at Glasgow revealed a dual strategy: on one hand, a willingness to contribute constructively to the global climate agenda by developing new frameworks for green finance and promoting sustainable technological innovation; on the other, a strong emphasis on fair burden-sharing between developed and developing nations. This stance highlights the growing awareness among BRICS countries of their crucial role in shaping global climate governance—not merely as recipients of policies, but as proactive actors in building a more inclusive and multipolar international order. The commitments made within the framework of COP26 also had a positive influence on the domestic environmental policies of BRICS members, fostering greater attention to the sustainable management of natural resources and the reduction of environmental degradation. Energy transition strategies, support for eco-friendly technologies, and the expansion of renewable energy sources have helped steer BRICS economies toward more resilient and sustainable models, although further efforts remain necessary to ensure consistency between declared objectives and actual outcomes (Fang, 2023).

COP27 – Sharm el-Sheikh, 2022

During the 2022 COP27 in Sharm el-Sheikh, the BRICS countries reaffirmed the importance of climate finance and a just transition to sustainable, low-carbon development. Regarding the just transition, the BRICS emphasized the need for a gradual and multi-level approach that recognizes the diverse national circumstances, with particular attention to the African context. They reiterated their support for the phased reduction of unabated coal and the elimination of inefficient fossil fuel subsidies, while encouraging the submission of new or updated NDCs and low-emission development strategies to ensure the concrete implementation of the Paris Agreement.

The joint statement of the BASIC group further reaffirmed the principle of CBDR, highlighting the need for enhanced financial and technological support for developing countries and the establishment of a fairer and more inclusive international financial system. The group also confirmed its commitment to strengthening national mitigation and adaptation policies, acknowledging the specific challenges faced by each country (Department of Forestry, Fisheries and the Environment, 2022).

COP28 – Dubai, 2023

At COP28 in Dubai, the BRICS countries reaffirmed their collective commitment to the implementation of the Paris Agreement, emphasizing the principles of the UNFCCC, particularly the principle of CBDR-RC. Their shared agenda centered on four main pillars: mitigation, adaptation, climate finance, and technology transfer. Each member underscored the urgency of coordinated action to address climate change while taking into account national circumstances and development priorities. Climate finance was reaffirmed as a cornerstone of the BRICS position. The group called on developed nations to increase financial support to developing countries to help them meet their mitigation and adaptation objectives. Brazil, in particular, emphasized the importance of creating financial mechanisms tailored to the differentiated needs of developing nations, thereby advancing principles of equity and climate justice. Alongside financing, technology transfer remains a strategic priority for the bloc. China's growing leadership in renewable energy innovation and investment—especially in solar, wind, and electric mobility—serves as a model for strengthening intra-BRICS cooperation and expanding access to sustainable technologies across the Global South (Singh, 2023).

In alignment with the UAE Consensus, the final COP28 outcome represented a significant, though ambiguous, milestone by acknowledging for the first time the need to transition away from fossil fuels. The conference also established the Loss and Damage Fund to support the most climate-vulnerable countries, marking a key step toward addressing global climate inequality. Moreover, the *Global Stocktake* highlighted the pressing need to reduce global greenhouse gas emissions by 43% by 2030 and by 60% by 2035, underscoring the necessity of equitable responsibilities, enhanced adaptation measures, and stronger financial and technological cooperation (BRICS Policy Center, 2024a).

Through these positions, the BRICS nations positioned themselves as a bridge between developed and developing countries, advocating for a balanced and inclusive approach to global climate governance—one that combines environmental sustainability, economic development, and social justice.

COP29 – Baku, 2024

The COP29 in Baku, held in November 2024, marked a significant moment for the BRICS group, as it was the first meeting in which the formation of BRICS Plus was officially recognized, with the initial countries joining the expanded framework. The BRICS expressed their commitment to the success of the conference through the Kazan Declaration, titled "*Strengthening Multilateralism for Just Development and Global Security.*" This declaration emphasized the need for concrete outcomes, particularly regarding climate finance for developing countries, advocating for a Quantified Collective Goal (QCG) of at least USD 1.3 trillion per year by 2035. The BRICS also expressed support for Brazil's role in hosting COP30 in 2025 and welcomed India's bid to host COP33 in 2028 (Abbasova, 2024; Borkena, 2024).

While COP29 produced several important outcomes, it also underscored significant challenges. Although the final agreement established the abovementioned QCG, this goal has been criticized by vulnerable countries as insufficient and for failing to prioritize public, grant-based financing. On the carbon market front, an agreement was reached on rules for implementing Article 6 of the Paris Agreement, governing the international transfer of mitigation outcomes and the establishment of a new international carbon market. Brazil announced new climate targets, committing to reduce CO_2 emissions by 59–67% by 2035 compared to 2005 levels; however, the Brazilian Climate Observatory highlighted a lack of ambition and clarity, particularly regarding deforestation policies. Another notable development was the establishment of the "Indigenous Peoples' Troika," composed of leaders from Brazil, Australia, and the Pacific Islands, aimed at strengthening indigenous participation in negotiations and promoting their rights. Civil society, however, criticized the overall outcomes of COP29, citing restrictions on freedom of expression and protest both inside and outside the conference (BRICS Policy Center, 2024b).

The BRICS also promoted the creation of a platform led by developing countries to align trade with sustainability objectives, emphasizing the importance of technology transfer and resilience-building as essential components of a more equitable global economy. Despite geopolitical challenges and divergences between developed and developing nations, the BRICS' position helped maintain a focus on climate justice and international solidarity. In conclusion, the participation of BRICS in COP29 reiterated their role as mediators between developed and developing countries, advancing a climate agenda that integrates environmental sustainability, economic development, and social justice, while reaffirming the importance of effective and inclusive multilateralism.

COP30 – Belém, 2025

The COP30 summit in Belém in November 2025 represented a pivotal moment for global climate governance, since, despite the usual criticisms and last-minute changes to targets, countries submitted updated NDCs following the *Global Stocktake* conducted at COP28. For the BRICS group, the summit had particular significance, coming shortly after the July 2025 BRICS summit in Rio de Janeiro, which demonstrated a renewed focus on climate action under Brazil's leadership. Brazil, hosting both the 2025 BRICS chairmanship and COP30, has played a central role, given its stewardship of the Amazon rainforest, which contains about 40% of the world's remaining tropical forests and stores roughly 200 billion tons of carbon. The country's initiatives—such as the Amazon Fund and its largely renewable electricity network—illustrate the intersection of climate resilience and social equity that the BRICS emphasize in their approach.

At the Rio summit, BRICS nations signaled a more assertive stance on climate issues, stressing coordinated action among major emerging economies. Key outcomes included an emphasis on enhanced climate finance, the development of green bond markets, and improved carbon accounting to ensure transparency in emissions reporting. The group also proposed a platform for aligning trade policies with sustainability objectives, reflecting an integrated approach to climate action. BRICS reaffirmed their commitment to protecting tropical forests, recognizing their central role in both biodiversity conservation and global carbon sequestration, and highlighted equity as a guiding principle in the transition toward low-carbon, climate-resilient economies. A particularly notable initiative endorsed by BRICS in 2025 is the creation of a fund aimed at conserving tropical forests. The fund is designed to generate approximately four billion dollars annually by combining public investments with private capital. This effort seeks to establish a sustainable financial model for forest protection, reinforcing the group's commitment to environmental stewardship and long-term climate stability. By linking conservation with sustainable development objectives, BRICS aim to support both ecological preservation and social resilience in forest-dependent regions.

In the lead-up to COP30, the BRICS countries also agreed on their first joint recommendation on climate finance, marking an important step in their collaborative strategy. The recommendation calls for reforms in multilateral development banks to better support climate initiatives and emphasizes mobilizing private capital to complement public funding. The BRICS stressed the importance of ensuring that climate finance is accessible, affordable, and timely for developing countries, aligning financial support with the principles of a just transition. This approach demonstrates the group's intention to provide practical tools for implementing climate commitments, particularly in the Global South. At COP30, the BRICS agenda was thus expected to center on translating promises into concrete action. The group's priorities include launching mechanisms such as the Tropical Forest Forever Facility, advancing plans to mobilize 1.3 trillion dollars annually in climate finance by 2035, and promoting inclusive governance through initiatives like the *Global Mutirão*, which engages indigenous communities, local governments, and civil society in climate decision-making. While the ambitions were high, the BRICS were aware of internal and external challenges, including conflicting domestic interests, logistical constraints, and a complex geopolitical environment shaped by the partial withdrawal of major developed economies from climate commitments (COP 30, 2025; BRICS, 2025a, 2025b; World Resources Institute, 2025).

Despite the BRICS' more proactive positioning at COP30, their practical commitments were still partial. The final declaration of the *Global Mutirão* (UNFCCC, 2025) reaffirmed the 1.5°C threshold set by the Paris Agreement, yet it offered no concrete mechanisms to achieve it. Fossil fuels were never mentioned explicitly, and the energy transition appeared only indirectly through a reference to the COP28 transitioning away from fossil fuels. No explicit call for a fossil-fuel phase-out was included, although new spaces for dialogue on emission reductions were opened, and a proposal was made to triple adaptation funding by 2035. While the BRICS continue to link environmental protection, social equity, and financial innovation—seeking to shape a collective, South-led approach to climate action—their position at COP30 fell short of endorsing a clearer and more ambitious commitment to phasing out fossil fuels, which still underpin much of their economic growth. Their emphasis on forest conservation, climate-finance reform, and inclusive governance signals a willingness to translate pledges into measurable outcomes and positions the BRICS as an increasingly influential actor in the evolving architecture of global climate policy. Nonetheless, more tangible short-term commitments were lacking. Moreover, the absence of the US from COP30 and the EU's eventual agreement to the existing text further underscore the declining leadership of Western actors in climate negotiations. This vacuum appears poised to be filled by the BRICS. Yet for the group to assume a credible leadership role, their future commitments will need to be more effective and concretely aligned with the urgency of the climate crisis.

References

Abbasova, N. (2024, October 23). BRICS expresses commitment to successful COP29 in Azerbaijan. *Report News Agency*. https://report.az/en/amp/cop29/brics-expresses-commitment-to-successful-cop29-in-azerbaijan.

Almeida, D. V., et al. (2023). The "Greening" of Empire: The European Green Deal as the EU first agenda. *Political Geography, 105*, 102925. https://doi.org/10.1016/j.polgeo.2023.102925

Amorim, A., Mattos, B., Santos, M., & Morales, P. (2015, October–November). The BRICS on the road to COP 21. *BPC Policy Brief*, 5(11). https://bricspolicycenter.org/wp-content/uploads/2015/11/BPC-Policy-Brief-5-11.pdf

Bhowmick, S. (2024, December 26). BRICS: Dopo le parole, i fatti. *ISPI Report*. https://www.ispionline.it/it/pubblicazione/brics-dopo-le-parole-i-fatti-195250

Birger Skjærseth, J., Guri, B., & Miranda, A. (2013). Explaining growing climate policy differences between the European Union and the United States. *Global Environmental Politics, 13*(4), 61–80. https://doi.org/10.1162/GLEP_a_00198

Borkena. (2024, November 19). BRICS climate collaboration at UN climate conference in Baku. https://borkena.com/2024/11/19/brics-climate-collaboration-at-un-climate-conference-in-baku/

BRICS. (2015a, April 22), Statement: First Official Meeting of BRICS Environment Ministers, Moscow, April 22. http://www.brics.utoronto.ca/docs/150422-environment.html.

BRICS Leaders Meeting. (2015b, July 09). The 7th BRICS Summit: Ufa Declaration, Russia. http://www.brics.utoronto.ca/docs/150709-ufa-declaration_en.html.

BRICS. (2022, May 24). Joint Statement Issued at the High-Level Meeting on Climate Change. http://brics2022.mfa.gov.cn/eng/hywj/ODMM/202205/t20220529_10694182.html

BRICS. (2025a, June 10). Ahead of COP30, BRICS approves first recommendation on climate finance. https://brics.br/en/news/brics-brasil-bulletin/12-ahead-of-cop30-brics-approves-first-recommendation-on-climate-finance

BRICS. (2025b, July 07). BRICS leaders champion global effort for fair climate finance in historic Rio Declaration. https://brics.br/en/brics-leaders-champion-global-effort-for-fair-climate-finance-in-historic-rio-declaration

BRICS Leaders Meeting. (2020, November 17). The 12th BRICS Summit: Moscow Declaration, "BRICS Partnership for Global Stability, Shared Security and Innovative Growth". http://www.brics.utoronto.ca/docs/201117-moscow-declaration.html

BRICS Policy Center. (2017). The 23rd Conference of the Parties of Climate Change (COP23). RADAR. https://bricspolicycenter.org/en/publications/the-23rd-conference-of-the-parties-of-climate-change-cop23/

BRICS Policy Center. (2022, October 31). COP 25 – Climate Change. https://bricspolicycenter.org/en/publications/cop-25-climate-change/.

BRICS Policy Center. (2024a, January 26). The outcomes of COP28. https://bricspolicycenter.org/en/the-outcomes-of-cop28/

BRICS Policy Center. (2024b, November 25). COP 29 results: Coverage of the BRICS Policy Center's Socio-Environmental Platform. https://bricspolicycenter.org/en/cop-29-results-coverage-of-the-brics-policy-centers-socio-environmental-platform/

Bruckmeier, K. (2024). *The anthropocene and its future the challenges of accelerating social and ecological change*. Palgrave Macmillan.

Brütsch, C., & Papa, M. (2013). Deconstructing the BRICS: Bargaining coalition, imagined community, or geopolitical fad? *The Chinese Journal of International Politics, 6*(3), 299–327.

Byiers, B., & Medinilla, A. (2024). The EU's Carbon Border Adjustment Mechanism and developing countries: Threats, opportunities and strategic responses. ECDPM, Discussion Paper No. 380. https://ecdpm.org/work/eus-carbon-border-adjustment-mechanism-and-developing-countries-threats-opportunities-and-strategic-responses

Center for Climate and Energy Solutions. (2011). Outcomes of the U.N. Climate Change Conference in Durban. https://www.c2es.org/wp-content/uploads/2011/12/outcomes-of-the-u-n-climate-change-conference-in-durban.pdf

Center for Climate and Energy Solutions. (2012, November 26). COP 18 Doha. https://www.c2es.org/content/cop-18-doha/

CGTN. (2024). Explainer: BRICS' role in global fight against climate change. https://news.cgtn.com/news/2024-10-21/Explainer-BRICS-role-in-global-fight-against-climate-change-1xRnLoLJOQo/p.html

Chapungu, L., Nhamo, G., Chikodzi, D., & Maoela, M. A. (2022). BRICS and the race to net-zero emissions by 2050: Is COVID-19 a barrier or an opportunity? *Journal of Open Innovation: Technology, Market, and Complexity, 8*(172), 1–20. https://doi.org/10.3390/joitmc8040172

Chatham House. (2021). Raising climate ambition at COP26. https://www.chathamhouse.org/2021/10/raising-climate-ambition-cop26/03-support-climate-vulnerable-developing-countries

Chevallier, R. (2011). COP17: What role for South Africa as an agent of change? Policy Briefing 38, November, Governance of Africa's Resources Programme. https://www.files.ethz.ch/isn/145969/saia_spb_38_chevallier_20111108.pdf?

Chime, V. (2023, August 17). CSOs: Africa Climate Summit Hijacked by Western Nations Pushing Hidden Agenda. *The Cable.* http://thecable.ng/csos-africa-climate-summit-hijacked-by-western-nations-pushing-hidden-agenda

Climate Action Tracker. (2025a). Russian Federation. Retrieved August 20, 2025, from https://climateactiontracker.org/countries/russian-federation/

Climate Action Tracker. (2025b). Retrieved August 20, 2025, from https://climateactiontracker.org/

COP30. (2025, July 08). BRICS leaders endorse unprecedented fund for conservation of tropical forests. https://cop30.br/en/news-about-cop30/brics-leaders-endorse-unprecedented-fund-for-conservation-of-tropical-forests

D'Souza, R. (2021, August 26). A Stocktaking of BRICS Performance in Climate Action. *ORF.* https://www.orfonline.org/research/a-stocktaking-of-brics-performance-in-climate-action

Department of Forestry, Fisheries and the Environment (DFFE). (2022, November 20). BASIC Ministerial joint statement at the UNFCCC's Sharm el-Sheikh Climate Change Conference (COP27/CMP17/CMA4). https://www.dffe.gov.za/index.php/BASIC-Ministerial-joint-statement-at-the-UNFCCC%E2%80%99s-Sharm-el-Sheikh-Climate-Change-Conference-%28COP27/CMP17/CMA4%29

Earth Negotiations Bulletin. (2022, November 20). Summary report, 6–20 November 2022. Sharm El-Sheikh Climate Change Conference-Intersessional Meetings. *International Institute for Environment and Development* (IIED). https://enb.iisd.org/sharm-el-sheikh-climate-change-conference-cop27-summary.

Fan, X. (2021). BRICS climate cooperation in the post-Paris Agreement era. *International Relations and Diplomacy, 9*(7), 259–277. https://doi.org/10.17265/2328-2134/2021.07.001

Fang, M. (2023). The role of COP26 commitment and technological innovation in depletion of natural resources: Evidence from BRICS countries. *Energy Policy, 177*, 113578. https://doi.org/10.1016/j.enpol.2023.113578

International Institute for Sustainable Development. (2018, July 27). BRICS Declaration Calls for Full Implementation of Paris Agreement and 2030 Agenda. *Sustainable Development Goals Knowledge Hub.* https://sdg.iisd.org/news/brics-declaration-calls-for-full-implementation-of-paris-agreement-and-2030-agenda/

Jacobs, M. (2014, December 16). What was the key achievement in Lima? World Economic Forum. https://www.weforum.org/stories/2014/12/what-was-the-key-achievement-in-lima/

Jinran, Z. (2017, June 24). BRICS pledges environment cooperation. *China Daily.* https://www.chinadaily.com.cn/china/2017-06/24/content_29869314.htm.

Linnér, B. O., & Pahuja, N. (2012). A registry of nationally appropriate mitigation actions: Goals, outcomes, and institutional requisites. *Ambio, 41*(1), 56–67. https://doi.org/10.1007/s13280-011-0241-6

Liquiang, H. (2023, September 09). BRICS plays role in global climate fight. *China Daily.* https://global.chinadaily.com.cn/a/202309/09/WS64fba0eda310d2dce4bb4c98.html?

Martinez, C. (2024). China's transition to an ecological civilization: Strategies and global implications. *International Critical Thought, 14*(2), 176–199. https://doi.org/10.1080/21598282.2024.2364311

Martuscelli, P. N., & Rinaldi, A. L. (2016). The BRICS on climate change global governance. *Meridiano., 47*(17), e17020. https://doi.org/10.20889/M47e17020

Ministry of Environment and Forests, Government of India. (2019, December 11). BASIC Ministerial Joint Statement at UNFCCC COP25. Government of India. https://www.pib.gov.in/newsite/PrintRelease.aspx?relid=195780

Ministry of External Affairs, Government of India. (2021, November 2). National Statement by Prime Minister Shri Narendra Modi at COP26 Summit in Glasgow. https://www.mea.gov.in/Speeches-Statements.htm?dtl%2F34466%2FNational+Statement+by+Prime+Minister+Shri+Narendra+Modi+at+COP26+Summit+in+Glasgow-

Naidoo, B. (2023, August 24). Towards a BRICS Climate Club. *Institute For Security Studies.* https://issafrica.org/iss-today/towards-a-brics-climate-club

Nair van Ryneveld, T., Phiri, B., & Simelan, K (2025, June 01). South Africa must take the lead in pan-African climate solidarity. *Mail & Guardian.* https://mg.co.za/thought-leader/opinion/2025-06-01-south-africa-must-take-the-lead-in-pan-african-climate-solidarity/

Omuko-Jung, L. A. (2014, November 24). The role of BRICS in future climate change regime: Why their commitment and participation is important and how to achieve it. *SSRN.* https://doi.org/10.2139/ssrn.2599248

Papagiannis, P. (2025). Ambição Climática dos BRICS: África do Sul. BPC PAPERS V.12. N. 01 - Janeiro/2025. Rio de Janeiro, PUC, BRICS Policy Center.

Qi, X. (2011). The rise of BASIC in UN climate change negotiations. *South African Journal of International Affairs, 18*(3), 295–318.

Republic of Moldova. (2013). The BRICS bloc of emerging economies at COP19 Warsaw. http://www.clima.md/libview.php?l=en&idc=76&id=3398

Saudi Vision 2030. (n.d.). Overview. Retrieved September, 28 2025, from https://www.vision2030.gov.sa/en/overview

Shen, Q., & Zou, X. (2024). Evolution of cooperation among BRICS countries in global climate governance: From UNFCCC to the Paris Agreement. *MGIMO*

Review of International Relations, 17(1), 65–85. https://doi.org/10.24833/2071-8160-2024-1-94-65-85

Sidiropoulos, E. (2024, November 29). A closer look at South Africa's approach to climate change and the G20. *South African Institute of International Affairs* (SAIIA). https://saiia.org.za/research/a-closer-look-at-south-africas-approach-to-climate-change-and-the-g20/

Singh, H. (2023, December 4). Bloc profile: BRICS at COP28. *Illuminem Voices.* https://illuminem.com/illuminemvoices/bloc-profile-brics-at-cop28

Solomon, H. (2024). BRICS Plus and climate change. In H. Solomon, S. Solomon, & B. Gupta (Eds.), *BRICS and Climate change: Balancing national interests, national development goals and global environmental sustainability* (pp. 165–181). Palgrave Macmillan.

Time for Africa. (2022, June 17). Cambiamenti Climatici in Sudafrica. https://timeforafrica.it/crediti-kwazulu-natal-provincial-government/.

Tshikovhi, N., et al. (Eds.). (2023). *COVID-19 and Climate Change in BRICS Nations: Beyond the Paris Agreement and Agenda 2030.* Routledge.

UNFCCC. (2010, March 30). Report of the Conference of the Parties on its fifteenth session, held in Copenhagen from 7 to 19 December 2009: Addendum — Part Two: Action taken by the Conference of the Parties (FCCC/CP/2009/11/Add.1). https://unfccc.int/resource/docs/2009/cop15/eng/11a01.pdf.

UNFCCC. (2013). Warsaw Framework for REDD+. https://redd.unfccc.int/fact-sheets/warsaw-framework-for-redd.html

UNFCCC. (2014). Lima call for climate action (Decision -/CP.20). https://unfccc.int/files/meetings/lima_dec_2014/application/pdf/auv_cop20_lima_call_for_climate_action.pdf

UNFCCC. (2025). Global Mutirão: Uniting humanity in a global mobilization against climate change. https://unfccc.int/sites/default/files/resource/Mutirão_cop30.pdf

UNFCCC. (n.d.-a). *Intro to Cancun Agreements.* https://unfccc.int/process/conferences/the-big-picture/milestones/the-cancun-agreements.

UNFCCC. (n.d.-b). *Cancun Agreements.* https://unfccc.int/process/conferences/pastconferences/cancun-climate-change-conference-november-2010/statements-and-resources/Agreements

White House. (2025, January 20). Putting America First in International Environmental Agreements. https://www.whitehouse.gov/presidential-actions/2025/01/putting-america-first-in-international-environmental-agreements/

World Bank. (2018). Climate Change Could Force Over 140 Million to Migrate Within Countries by 2050: World Bank Report. https://www.worldbank.org/en/news/press-release/2018/03/19/climate-change-could-force-over-140-million-to-migrate-within-countries-by-2050-world-bank-report

World Resources Institute. (2025, July 07). Statement: BRICS countries rally around assertive climate agenda ahead of COP30. https://www.wri.org/news/statement-brics-countries-rally-around-assertive-climate-agenda-ahead-cop30

CHAPTER 7

New Technologies and International Security

Abstract This chapter explores the evolving role of the BRICS (Brazil, Russia, India, China, and South Africa) in reshaping global security, technological innovation, and international governance amid the shifting geopolitical context of the mid-2020s. Once conceived primarily as an economic alliance, the BRICS have progressively expanded their agenda to include new domains—most notably security, artificial intelligence (AI), and defense cooperation—positioning themselves as an emerging pole of influence within a multipolar world order. Against the backdrop of Donald Trump's renewed presidency and his "America First" policies, this expansion has acquired renewed significance, as the group seeks to consolidate internal cohesion and strategic autonomy in the face of heightened global instability. The chapter traces the institutional evolution of BRICS cooperation in Science, Technology, and Innovation (STI), beginning with the 2011 Sanya Summit and the 2015 Memorandum of Understanding on STI, which established a framework for collaboration on issues such as AI, renewable energy, nanotechnology, and space research. The analysis highlights how these initiatives have enabled the BRICS to position themselves as normative actors in global science governance, particularly through the 2024 Kazan Declaration and the 2025 Leaders' Declaration on the Global Governance of Artificial Intelligence. These documents underscore the bloc's ambition to promote equitable access to technology, protect digital sovereignty, and prevent new forms of "digital colonialism" that risk

F. Petrone, *The BRICS and the Transformation of Global Power*,
https://doi.org/10.1007/978-3-032-23540-4_7

deepening inequalities between the Global North and South. At the same time, the chapter examines the growing security dimension of BRICS cooperation, characterized by increased defense spending, military modernization, and joint exercises—especially between China and Russia—alongside persistent intra-group rivalries such as those between India and China. Through platforms like the Shanghai Cooperation Organization and the newly created BRICS Nuclear Energy Platform, the bloc is gradually institutionalizing its strategic and security agenda, emphasizing multilateralism, non-intervention, and respect for sovereignty. Finally, the chapter situates the BRICS within the broader system of global governance, contrasting their cooperative, development-oriented approach with NATO's collective defense model. By invoking the legacy of the Non-Aligned Movement, the BRICS aim to articulate an alternative vision of global order—one grounded in pluralism, technological inclusivity, and balanced power relations. The chapter concludes that the BRICS' ability to overcome internal divergences and translate normative aspirations into practical governance mechanisms will be decisive for the future of global security and technological governance.

Keywords BRICS • BRICS Universities League • Artificial intelligence • Security cooperation • Technological innovation • NATO

Introduction

The emergence of the BRICS has had decisive influences in several areas, as we have seen, ranging from the economy to geopolitics, climate negotiations, and South–South cooperation. At the same time, the group—originally conceived as an economic alliance—has gradually expanded its reach into the fields of security and new technologies. These areas are truly essential, and the BRICS' growing presence in them demonstrates their vital importance on the international stage. Indeed, the rapid pace of technological innovation within the BRICS countries is having profound implications for international cooperation, economic development, and global security. More broadly, the group's expanding influence in these domains is already shaping global geopolitics and decision-making, and will continue to shape them in the years ahead.

However, the recent re-election of Donald Trump for a new presidential term in the US introduces greater complexity into the international scene. His America First policy, combined with increased tariffs and a more isolationist approach, has altered relations among major powers and impacted the strategies of the BRICS, who are being forced to reorient their policies toward greater cooperation among themselves. The most emblematic image of this shift was undoubtedly the meeting between Indian Prime Minister Modi, Russian President Putin, and Chinese President Xi during the SCO Summit in Tianjin in 2025, where the leaders called for a "true multilateralism" and outlined the prospects for a new global order.

Although tensions with Russia have long been evident, and rivalry with China—especially in the economic sphere but not limited to it—has intensified to the point of evoking the notion of a new Cold War, straining relations with Beijing has undoubtedly proven to be a risky move for the US This is primarily due to economic reasons, as clearly demonstrated during the Asia-Pacific Economic Cooperation summit held in Gyeongju, South Korea, in late October 2025. During this meeting, President Trump was forced to backtrack on his plan to impose new tariffs on Chinese products, aware that such a decision would have had significant repercussions for the US economy. One of the key issues concerns the so-called rare earth elements (REEs)—critical minerals essential for the production of a wide range of technological devices—of which China is the world's largest holder and upon which the US is heavily dependent (BBC News, 2025; Xinghui, 2025). According to the Mineral Commodity Summaries 2025 published by the US Geological Survey, China, Brazil, India, and Russia rank among the top five countries in global REE reserves, while South Africa occupies the tenth position (US Geological Survey, 2025). This configuration places the BRICS group in a position of dominance within the global rare earth market.

Beyond the economic dimension, other factors also come into play. For instance, India—once regarded as a key strategic partner for the US in Asia—has entered a phase of uncertainty in its bilateral relations with Washington, following the American government's decision to impose 50% tariffs on Indian goods. This has, in turn, prompted India to seek new partnerships, as the country grows increasingly skeptical about the reliability of its ties with Washington. Such tensions also risk undermining the Quadrilateral Security Dialogue (Quad)—the strategic forum comprising India, Australia, Japan, and the US—originally established in 2007 to serve as a counterbalance to China's rise (Mehta, 2025; Nanda, 2025).

A similar analysis applies to Brazil and South Africa. In the case of Brazil, the US imposed 50% tariffs, which President Trump at times justified on the grounds that former President Jair Bolsonaro had been subjected to political persecution by the current government of Luiz Inácio Lula da Silva, leading to his imprisonment. Beyond these ostensible political reasons, however, there is a significant geopolitical dimension: Brazil's continued membership in BRICS and, more broadly, a political vision that is largely incompatible with that of the current Republican US administration (Aguirre Ernst, 2025).

Tensions with South Africa have also been notable. On May 21, 2025, President Trump hosted President Cyril Ramaphosa at the White House, during which he screened a video claiming to show a "genocide" against white farmers in South Africa, thereby promoting an unfounded conspiracy theory and exacerbating bilateral tensions. Yet, this incident reflects deeper issues, such as Pretoria's growing closeness to countries like Russia and Iran, which help explain both this episode and, more broadly, the current US administration's economic and political policies toward South Africa (Gavin, 2025; De Guzman & Schneid, 2025).

In any case, all these events—both sudden and, in many respects, surprising, and likely marking the beginning of a new phase in the global order—have highlighted the need for the BRICS countries to develop more independent and effective governance in matters of security and technological innovation, thereby strengthening their decision-making autonomy and internal cohesion.

The Role of New Technologies, Global Security, and Cooperation between the BRICS and the Global South

The origins of BRICS collaboration in the field of Information and Communication Technologies (ICT) can be traced back to the broader framework of Science, Technology, and Innovation (STI) cooperation. This cooperation, guided by the BRICS vision of strengthening partnerships for common development and deepening collaborative efforts, was first articulated at the 3rd BRICS Summit, held in Sanya, China, in 2011. Rooted in the principles of voluntary participation, equality, mutual benefit, and reciprocity, this framework emphasized people-centered and public-good–oriented STI as a key instrument to foster equitable growth and sustainable development across member states (International Cooperation Division, 2015). Building upon these foundations, on March 18, 2015, the BRICS countries signed a Memorandum of Understanding (MoU) on STI in Brasília, which formalized their commitment to advancing joint initiatives in STI and laid the groundwork for subsequent sectoral collaborations, including in ICT. This MoU established a strategic framework for collaboration in STI aimed at tackling shared socio-economic and developmental challenges. Grounded in principles of voluntary participation, equality, mutual benefit, and respect for national sovereignty, it seeks to foster sustainable development, innovation, and knowledge exchange among BRICS members, positioning STI as a key pillar of intra-BRICS cooperation. The agreement identifies several priority areas, including food security, climate change and disaster management, renewable energy, nanotechnology, biotechnology and health, high-performance computing, and space research. Cooperation is implemented through joint research projects, multilateral funding mechanisms, researcher exchanges, training programs, and shared research infrastructure, all guided by three-year work plans that set priorities and track progress. Coordination takes place through regular BRICS ministerial meetings on STI and is further supported by initiatives such as the BRICS Research and Innovation Initiative and the BRICS GRAIN platform. The MoU's overarching goal is to strengthen scientific integration, enhance innovation capacity, and consolidate the BRICS as a collective actor in global science governance. At the same time, it acknowledges key challenges, including disparities in capacities and resources among member states and the need for effective coordination mechanisms. Thus, the 2015 BRICS STI MoU represents an important step toward a more inclusive and cooperative global innovation system, driven by emerging powers committed to sustainable and shared progress (BRICS, 2015). Another important legal act adopted in 2015 is the BRICS Economic Partnership Strategy, which aims to strengthen the growth and competitiveness of the BRICS countries by focusing on the digital and innovative economy. The Strategy promotes the development of advanced technologies, skills training, and the building of knowledge-based economies, while ensuring a safe and cooperative digital environment. It recognizes the key role of ICT, such as artificial intelligence (AI) and the Internet of Things, while also addressing risks related to security and data protection. The Strategy foresees cooperation among BRICS countries on standards, technologies, connectivity costs, and human capital development—objectives that were further reaffirmed in the Goa Declaration of 2016 (Cyman et al., 2021).

A key milestone came with the 2017 Xiamen Declaration in China, where the BRICS leaders made their first explicit reference to AI, emphasizing the need to expand and institutionalize cooperation in this rapidly evolving sector (Mahrenbach & Papa, 2024). In subsequent summits, the BRICS countries have consistently highlighted—directly or indirectly—the importance of cooperation in the field of STI. This sustained attention demonstrates a shared commitment to advancing STI collaboration. The BRICS view AI as a key instrument for economic growth, development, technological progress, and more inclusive societies, with references to collaboration and progress frequently appearing as central elements in their statements on AI. However, during the COVID-19 pandemic, as member states shifted their focus toward recovery efforts, STI initiatives were somewhat deprioritized, even though some initiatives did emerge during this period, for example, bilateral investments in AI, such as the $1 billion Russia–China Technology Investment Fund established in 2021(Mahrenbach & Papa, 2024). Later, in 2025, another bilateral agreement was signed between China and Brazil on the sidelines of the annual BRICS conference in Rio de Janeiro, aiming to advance technology transfer, promote well-being, and integrate technologies into machinery for environmental and soil monitoring (Pessarlay, 2025).

In any case, STI regained a central role during the 2023 summit, which implemented AI policies and advanced members' AI capabilities. It was at this summit that the BRICS AI Study Group and the Digital Economy Working Group were created, aiming to develop "digital education cooperative mechanisms" (Mahrenbach & Papa, 2024). From this point onward, initiatives to deepen technological cooperation and reinforce BRICS collaboration in AI specifically began to gain momentum again.

Indeed, the 16th BRICS Summit in Kazan, Russia, in 2024 represented an important milestone. The document related to the "Kazan Declaration" addressed issues concerning technology and global security, emphasizing the importance of enhancing international cooperation. In particular, it recognized that rapid technological changes, including the advancement of AI, offer new opportunities for overall socio-economic development, and encouraged broader international discussion on the topic, supporting the role of the United Nations in the global governance of AI. To this end, the UN General Assembly Resolution A/RES/78/311, which promotes international cooperation in AI capacity-building, is welcomed. Specifically, points 78, 79, 80, and 81 of the Declaration are dedicated to new technologies, security, and innovation. These points highlight the importance of closing the digital divide and ensuring equitable access to ICTs as tools for sustainable development. The commitment to promoting cooperation in cybersecurity and maintaining an open, secure, and stable ICT environment is reaffirmed. Another crucial point is the need to strengthen international cooperation to prevent the use of ICT technologies in criminal or terrorist activities, while respecting human rights and fundamental freedoms. Finally, the importance of promoting technological innovation and digital transformation in productive sectors is emphasized, as a driver of economic growth, job creation, and sustainable development (BRICS, 2024). These points reflect the BRICS countries' attention to the challenges and opportunities related to new technologies and global security, with particular emphasis on the central role of the United Nations and the need for international cooperation in these areas. Emerging technologies, particularly AI, are playing a crucial role in the economic development and geopolitical dynamics of the BRICS. Although these countries show significant differences in terms of technological development and industrial capacity, they share a common vision: to leverage new technologies to strengthen their global economic competitiveness and reduce dependence on traditional economic models dominated by Western powers.

The most recent, XVII BRICS Summit, held in Rio de Janeiro in July 2025, was also a pivotal event regarding the bloc's interest in emerging technologies, particularly AI. The joint declaration issued at the summit included 126 commitments covering areas such as global governance, finance, health, climate change, and, for the first time, AI (BRICS, 2025a). Notably, the summit released the *Leaders' Declaration on Global Governance of Artificial Intelligence*, also adopted on July 6, 2025, marking a significant step in the BRICS countries' efforts to position themselves as normative actors in this strategic field. The document acknowledges AI's transformative potential for economic and social development, while also highlighting global risks such as digital inequalities, concentration of technological power, misuse for military or surveillance purposes, and lack of algorithmic transparency. In response, BRICS leaders call for the establishment of a multilateral AI governance framework grounded in equity, technological sovereignty, ethical responsibility, and international cooperation. They emphasize the need to ensure fair access to emerging technologies, especially for countries in the Global South, in order to prevent new forms of digital colonialism and reduce the technological gap between the Global North and South. The declaration further proposes the creation of intergovernmental coordination mechanisms, the development of shared standards, and active participation in global regulatory processes, particularly within the UN, to foster inclusive and pluralistic governance (BRICS, 2025a).

In this respect, the BRICS approach presents an alternative to the models promoted by the US and the EU, which are primarily market-driven or regulation-centered, respectively. While BRICS emphasizes technological sovereignty, multilateral cooperation, and equitable participation of Global South countries, the EU and the US follow trajectories shaped by different institutional traditions and priorities. The BRICS joint declaration stresses principles such as fair access to technology, transparency, cultural inclusion, and autonomous development, recognizing that existing governance models are often Western-centered and may marginalize less technologically advanced countries (BRICS, 2025b; CADE Project, 2025). In contrast, the EU has implemented the AI Act, introducing binding rules, risk classifications, transparency requirements, human oversight, data protection, accountability, and legal controls. The US has historically taken a more flexible approach: under President Joe Biden, governance relied on executive orders, voluntary guidelines and standards, sectoral initiatives, and innovation incentives, maintaining regulatory flexibility to encourage growth and competitiveness (Jelinek, 2024; Fauchoux & Perissinotto, 2023). In 2025, the Trump administration pursued a market-driven model aimed at strengthening American leadership through shared infrastructure, private investment incentives, and a dynamic tech sector. US governance emphasizes technical standards, regulatory sandboxes, and monitoring tools such as the AI Information Sharing and Analysis Center to track security risks, while avoiding overly restrictive legislation. Particular attention is given to workforce training, talent attraction, and international collaboration to consolidate the US position in the global AI market (Meinhardt et al., 2025; The White House, 2025). For the BRICS, a central concern is preventing AI governance from becoming a tool of normative dominance by technologically advanced countries. The EU and the US, in contrast, each aim to influence global rules according to their respective models: the EU through binding regulation and human-rights-centered ethics, and the US through innovation leadership and international influence. The BRICS vision thus reflects the ambition to construct a multipolar technological order, where AI rules reflect a plurality of values, traditions, and national priorities.

Recent months have seen concrete steps to strengthen cooperation beyond the Rio Summit. On January 3, 2025, the China-BRICS Artificial

Intelligence Development and Cooperation Center was inaugurated in Shanghai, intended to become a strategic hub for AI innovation. The facility hosts 34 large-scale AI models and China's first community dedicated to large AI models, Mosu (Model Speed Space), which has attracted around 100 startups. During the inauguration, startup representatives highlighted opportunities arising from the restructuring of global supply chains and the importance of the BRICS market, noting how advanced language models can facilitate international collaboration. The center aims to strengthen AI cooperation among BRICS countries and foster global technological development (China Association for Science and Technology, 2025). In 2025, the NDB also launched the Digital Sovereignty Fund, a $5 billion initiative to strengthen AI-related infrastructure, including research parks, data centers, and chip production capabilities. This initiative underscores the NDB's commitment to fully embracing AI and promoting excellence and leadership for the Global South (Think BRICS, 2025).

However, despite the coherence of the principles expressed, the numerous declarations and initiatives launched, and undoubtedly the significant economic efforts that the BRICS are investing in the AI sector, several challenges remain. These include the absence of binding mechanisms, internal disparities in technological capabilities, political divergences among members, and differing national priorities. For instance, China has invested substantial resources in AI, aiming to become a global leader in this field by 2030. Russia, still lagging behind China in technological capacity, is seeking to close this gap by focusing on emerging technologies such as quantum computing and cybersecurity. In India and South Africa, AI is being applied to address local challenges, such as improving access to education and healthcare, and to foster innovation within small and medium-sized enterprises. Although efforts are officially made to reconcile these differences, they raise questions about the BRICS' real capacity to translate this vision into an effective and coordinated operational model. This task is further complicated by the BRICS Plus strategy and the inclusion of new members, who in some cases face significant gaps compared to the five core BRICS, particularly China. Nevertheless, the declarations, policy positions, and evolving AI governance within BRICS serve to strengthen the group's role in global governance and stimulate broader debates on the need for a multipolar, inclusive, and cooperative approach to regulating emerging technologies.

In this context, new technologies—AI in particular—represent not only an opportunity to enhance partnerships among these countries, promoting the exchange of resources and expertise, but also a bridge toward the Global South, facilitating cooperation beyond traditional power centers (Goswami, 2024), encouraging greater inclusion within the context of South–South cooperation and providing a means of sharing knowledge with countries in the Global South, which suffer from a significant gap in this area—a gap that has repercussions in other domains as well, such as their capacity to tackle climate change.

Thus, the BRICS are investing in joint development programs and creating platforms for collaboration in advanced research, with a particular focus on AI applications in health, manufacturing, and cybersecurity. An example of this cooperation is also the creation of shared research centers that promote the transfer of technologies and skills among the nations, having a positive impact on global growth and security. In this sense, initiatives related to partnerships between universities are particularly interesting. In particular, in 2013, under the initiative of Fudan University in Shanghai, the BRICS University League was created—a consortium of leading universities and research centers in BRICS countries that serves as a platform for academic cooperation, research, and international projects. Recently, this format has also been extended to countries that have joined or are joining BRICS Plus, resulting in the creation of the BRICS+ University Association, a non-profit alliance that supports universities by facilitating international cooperation in higher education and creating opportunities for meetings, networking, and dialogue (BRICS Plus Universities Association, n.d.).

Through these initiatives, there is a clear intention to further expand and strengthen cooperation in the field of education; however, in carrying out this effort, the BRICS Plus countries are also placing special value on new technologies and innovations such as AI. These countries are well aware of the diplomatic and geopolitical implications of technological leadership, and therefore, initiatives in this area are expected to increase in the coming years. Specifically regarding AI, the BRICS are fully aware that this emerging technological field is fundamental for future challenges and plays an essential role in redefining global security. In the specific case of the Global South, as we have noted, the BRICS are advocating for this part of the world to have a greater voice in matters related to new technologies (Xinyi, 2024). At the same time they are launching a series of initiatives aimed at strengthening their digital sovereignty and reducing dependence on Silicon Valley-centered digital ecosystems (Jiang & Belli, 2024).

Moreover, aside from the fact that new technologies are not equally accessible to all countries, they are having significant repercussions on the labor market. In particular, besides creating new jobs, it appears that large multinational corporations operating in the Internet sector have a strong need to outsource their production and, consequently, reduce production costs. In a way, at least in this respect, it is telling that Big Tech industries—especially Western ones—have a major interest in seeking cheap labor, particularly in the poorest areas of the world, thereby reproducing, in some ways, the *modus operandi* of (almost) all industries in advanced capitalism. It is no coincidence, therefore, that many Big Tech companies, especially those from the US, are outsourcing their services to markets such as Sub-Saharan Africa and Southeast Asia, and more generally to the Global South, where labor costs are lower, attempting to impose a true "digital colonialism" (Kwet, 2019).

Thus, in this regard, the initiatives promoted by the BRICS, particularly in AI governance, could serve as a further impetus to draw greater attention also to labor conditions in these regions of the world.

An Overview of the Development of AI National Strategies in the BRICS (Plus) Countries

Looking more specifically at the main initiatives of the individual countries in the field of new technologies, we can observe how China, under the leadership of President Xi Jinping, is striving to assume a dominant role not only in industrial production but also in new technologies. China has developed cutting-edge digital infrastructures and invested massively in AI, blockchain, and big data projects. These investments are part of a broader strategic plan to reduce technological dependence on the West and strengthen its geopolitical position. Also noteworthy is the so-called Digital Silk Road initiative. Launched in 2015, it represents an effort by China to expand its digital influence across the world. The Digital Silk Road is part of the larger Belt and Road Initiative—the world's largest infrastructure project—and has become a significant component of China's global strategy. Through it, China offers various forms of assistance to recipient countries. As part of this broader project, the Digital Silk Road also supports Chinese exporters, including many well-known tech companies such as Huawei, aiming to improve telecommunications networks, AI capabilities, cloud computing, e-commerce, mobile payment systems, and other high-tech sectors in the recipient countries (Council on Foreign Relations, 2021). Of course, there are critics who view this initiative as an attempt by China to become the undisputed global leader in technology, using its dominant position to impose new forms of digital colonialism (Rosano, 2024).

Russia, although possessing lower technological capabilities than China, has recognized new technologies as a fundamental resource to counter economic sanctions and increase its influence on the international stage. Cooperation between China and Russia on technological issues is expected to grow, with the BRICS bloc serving as a platform to accelerate technological progress and promote common governance. It is emblematic that President Putin, aware of the impact new technologies will have on the global system, has stated that whoever dominates AI will dominate the world (Haski, 2017). Putin has also reiterated the importance of greater cooperation with the BRICS group to jointly develop new technologies, and in particular, to benefit from the use of AI (Bryanski, 2024). Moreover, Russia is also encouraging cooperation with the new members that have joined and will join the BRICS through the BRICS Plus strategy (Irina Dezhina, 2024). More specifically, Russia's AI initiatives officially began in 2018 with the "Digital Economy" program, which allocated funds for digitalization, focusing on end-to-end digital technologies, cybersecurity, and infrastructures. The program involved Sberbank, Russia's main state-owned bank, which was tasked with developing a roadmap for AI and neurotechnology. In 2019, Sberbank drafted a national strategy on AI, approved that same year, which sets the guidelines for AI development through 2030. In addition, the Russian government created a "regulatory sandbox" to encourage innovation, allowing for experimentation with AI. Russia's AI ecosystem is led by Sberbank, which also founded the AI Research Institute and the AI Russia Alliance. Other key players include Rostec, with a particular focus on the defense sector, and Yandex, the largest private tech company. Other significant actors are Gazprom Neft and Skolkovo, a technology center that hosts startups and research on AI (Geohistory, 2022). AI is also an important topic for the Russian military sector, with the use of this technology for data management and the enhancement of defense systems. The war with Ukraine was the first major conflict characterized by a more widespread use of AI, where Ukraine, supported by American companies, countered Russian attacks, forcing

Russia to intensify the use of AI in command systems, drones, and air defense.

Russia began taking an interest in AI in the 1960s, but the acceleration in investments came after the annexation of Crimea in 2014, with the formulation of national strategies and investments to modernize the military with advanced technologies. The use of AI in the military domain has become a central focus, with more than 500 active AI projects in the Russian defense industry by 2023. The integration of AI into drones and air defense systems has improved the effectiveness of the armed forces, with the introduction of new technologies such as the HX-2 drones used in Ukraine. Investment in AI could help reduce Russia's technological gap with China and the US, although experts acknowledge that Russia still lags behind in terms of capability. Nevertheless, the war in Ukraine has provided Russia with direct experience in the use of AI in a real conflict. Moreover, cooperation with other states could foster the development of new capabilities in this sector, with potential geopolitical implications. Internationally, cooperation with China and South Korea, to mention two examples, is very active, with Huawei and Samsung leading research projects (Sukhankin, 2025). Despite a late start, Russia has made significant progress in AI development, thanks to national initiatives and international cooperation.

India, for its part, has launched a series of strategic initiatives to promote the development and integration of AI across various sectors, within the broader framework of the "IndiaAI Mission." This national strategy aims to harness the potential of AI for economic growth and social welfare.Among the main initiatives are the *INDIAai* and *Bhashini* platforms. *INDIAai*, launched in May 2020, is the national AI portal, providing resources, news, and updates about the sector in India. *Bhashini*, introduced in August 2022, focuses on eliminating language barriers through translation services across India's diverse languages, thus promoting digital inclusion. The government has also allocated significant funding to the IndiaAI Mission program, aiming to create a favorable ecosystem for the development of AI in key sectors such as health, agriculture, and education. Investments include strengthening AI infrastructure and supporting startups, in order to stimulate innovation and address social challenges. The launch of strategic portals like *INDIAai* and *Bhashini*, along with other initiatives such as BharatGen, demonstrates India's proactive approach to adopting AI. These efforts seek to position the country as a key player in the global AI landscape, promoting innovation, digital inclusion, and economic development (AI Certs, 2025).

With the ambitious Brazilian Artificial Intelligence Plan (*Plano Brasileiro de Inteligência Artificial* -PBIA) 2024–2028, launched in July 2024, Brazil presented its strategy on AI and new technologies. Titled "AI for the Good of All," the plan aims to make Brazil a global leader in AI by promoting sustainable and socially oriented technologies. The strategy includes investments in advanced computing infrastructures and resources, inclusive training programs, AI applications to improve public services, support for business innovation, and a regulatory framework for the ethical use of artificial intelligence. The plan has a budget of 23.03 billion reais (approximately 4 billion dollars) distributed over four years. Most of the funds will be allocated to supporting businesses, creating national data centers, and developing the AI ecosystem, while over 5 billion reais will finance infrastructure and sustainable energy projects for AI. The remainder will be used for training initiatives, improvement of public services, and regulation of the sector (Ministério da Ciência, Tecnologia e Inovações, 2024).

South Africa's current AI strategy is based on two government initiatives: the Centre for Artificial Intelligence Research (CAIR), established in 2011 to support academic research, and the AI Institute of South Africa (AIISA), founded in 2022 to develop AI applications in the public and private sectors. In 2024, the Department of Communications and Digital Technologies (DCDT) published a discussion paper during the National Government AI Summit, identifying four strategic priorities: promoting an inclusive AI agenda, investing in training, studying policies to mitigate the negative effects of AI, and incentivizing economic growth through investments in the sector. The goals for 2030 include training 5000 AI experts, improving basic skills in 30% of the workforce, creating 100 to 300 AI startups, and attracting direct investments of 70 billion rands. The summit also led to the publication of South Africa's AI Policy Framework, the first step toward a national strategy, which aims to address internal challenges and seize economic opportunities. The framework proposes an approach called the Futures Triangle (Gumede, 2024), which considers current technological advances (Push of the Present), national development goals (Pull of the Future), and the country's historical inequalities (Weight of the Past).

The New BRICS Strategies on AI

Regarding the new BRICS member states—those that officially joined the group following the implementation of the BRICS Plus strategy—it is possible to observe a growing effort to integrate AI into their national development plans. Despite this commitment, these countries still face significant challenges related to inclusive governance, protection of digital rights, and the reduction of technological inequalities. However, the strategies adopted by the new BRICS members demonstrate a clear and increasing engagement with AI as a key instrument for economic and social transformation.

In Egypt, both the Vision 2030 and the National AI Strategy outline the ambition to position the country as a regional AI hub, with targeted initiatives in education, healthcare, transportation, and smart cities. Membership in BRICS reinforces this trajectory, supported by significant investments in research infrastructure and smart governance. Nonetheless, persistent issues remain, including limited civic participation and territorial inequalities in access to digital technologies.

In Ethiopia, the Digital Ethiopia 2025 strategy reflects the government's intention to foster inclusive development driven by AI, despite fragile digital infrastructure and political instability. The Ethiopian Artificial Intelligence Institute plays a central role in research and capacity building. However, challenges such as centralized information control, frequent network disruptions, and restricted civic freedoms hinder the establishment of a genuinely inclusive AI governance framework.

Similarly, Iran, operating under the constraints of international sanctions, views AI as a means of modernization and self-sufficiency. Its National Artificial Intelligence Strategy emphasizes research, education, and industrial partnerships, while recent large-scale national projects aim to strengthen energy resilience and infrastructure capacity. Nevertheless, issues related to censorship, lack of transparency, and limited civil society participation undermine the development of open and inclusive governance mechanisms.

The United Arab Emirates stand out for their globally oriented AI strategy. The UAE Artificial Intelligence Strategy 2031 promotes rapid innovation and digital transformation, supported by an advanced regulatory framework and dedicated institutions such as the Ministry of Artificial Intelligence and the UAE AI Office. The main applications are concentrated in the healthcare sector, including remote patient monitoring, personalized treatment plans, and advanced diagnostic systems. Yet, concerns persist regarding data privacy and the employment impact of automation.

Indonesia, a new member of the BRICS Network University, is increasingly investing in AI for education. With the fourth largest education system in the world, the country considers AI essential to improving teaching quality. Major initiatives include the Rumah Pendidikan national platform for personalized learning and the introduction of AI and programming curricula in thousands of schools (Think BRICS, 2025).

Finally, Saudi Arabia is implementing an ambitious AI strategy that seeks to redefine the nation's structure and global role, aiming to become a worldwide hub for AI. The ultimate goal is to make AI a core infrastructure for economic and social transformation, rather than a stand-alone sector. This vision follows a systemic and anticipatory approach: first building the foundations—digital infrastructure, regulation, training, and investment—and then fostering an innovative ecosystem capable of operating globally. Projects such as NEOM serve as experimental laboratories for testing integrated AI solutions in smart urban environments. The Saudi strategy also seeks to position the country as a leading global provider of compute-as-a-service for emerging markets in Africa and Asia, effectively becoming the infrastructural backbone of AI ecosystems in developing regions. The Public Investment Fund (PIF), with over $900 billion in assets, has already allocated more than $40 billion to AI-related initiatives, including HumAIn, the national platform for AI infrastructure. Unlike other national programs focused mainly on software and algorithms, Saudi Arabia is investing heavily in the physical foundations of AI: energy, data centers, semiconductors, and connectivity (Falk, 2025; Soliman, 2025).

The Future of BRICS and Emerging Technologies

Looking to the future, the BRICS bloc is therefore set to become an increasingly important player in the field of emerging technologies (Baschuk, 2023). With the expansion of its members and the integration of new economies, the group will have the opportunity to further increase its global market share and shape the future of the digital economy. However, for BRICS to become true leaders in the technology sector, it will be crucial to further strengthen internal policies and strengthen a common vision, not only in the economic realm but also in the regulatory, political, and cultural spheres. In this context, emerging technologies such as AI, blockchain, and quantum computing present an unprecedented opportunity for the BRICS countries to redefine the rules of global competitiveness and foster a more equitable world order, in which the Global South can play a more central role.

The future prospects of BRICS, in relation to new technologies, also have significant implications for the fight against climate change. In fact, the group is focusing on the use of digital technologies to improve the effectiveness of climate initiatives. The member countries of the group, apart from AI, are also promoting digital innovation by investing in blockchain and the Internet of Things (IoT)—tools that can enhance the monitoring, reporting, and verification (MRV) of climate actions, thereby increasing transparency and accountability. Additionally, the creation of a digital platform for the exchange of climate data between member states is being explored to improve policy coordination and the implementation of common initiatives.

Another key aspect refers to the use of digital technologies to raise public awareness about climate change and promote sustainable practices, leveraging social media and mobile applications to engage with citizens and encourage climate-friendly actions. BRICS has also shown a growing interest in the development and adoption of new technologies to strengthen economic cooperation and reduce dependence on Western financial systems. Its strategy is based on the already mentioned South–South cooperation, with a strong commitment to technology transfer and knowledge exchange, especially in the renewable energy sector. Countries like China and India, leaders in solar energy, promote initiatives such as the International Solar Alliance and are among the world's leading producers of solar panels and electric vehicles, offering advantageous economic solutions to partner countries. Furthermore, BRICS is involved in joint research programs on emerging technologies such as hydrogen, battery storage, and smart grids, fostering collaboration among its members and with partner nations.

There are also other initiatives that reflect the BRICS' intention to establish a more independent framework, free from Western dominance. Among these technological measures is BRICS Pay, a decentralized payment system launched in 2018, designed to facilitate transactions between member countries using local currencies and to reduce reliance on the US dollar. This system helps promote financial inclusion by reducing costs and complexity in international transactions. Another initiative is the abovementioned Artificial Intelligence Alliance, announced in December 2024 by Russia in collaboration with other BRICS countries and nations like Serbia and Indonesia. This alliance aims to promote joint research, AI regulation, and access to markets for products based on this technology, with the intention of challenging the dominance of the US in the sector and strengthening the position of the BRICS (Bryanski, 2024).

Additionally, during the BRICS summit in October 2024, several proposals were presented to strengthen the economic independence of the group through the use of new technologies. Apart from the aforementioned BRICS Cross-Border Payments Initiative—which envisions the development of a new payment system based on national currencies and blockchain technology to enhance security and eliminate the need for dollar-based transactions—another significant proposal is the creation of BRICS Clear, an international infrastructure for payment clearing and settlement that ensures continued access to BRICS financial markets even in the event of exclusion from Western systems. The creation of BRICS Reinsurance, a reinsurance company to ensure continuous trade between BRICS countries regardless of Western reinsurance services, was also proposed, along with strengthening cooperation in credit rating assessments, using AI to eliminate biases and protect BRICS markets from the withdrawal of Western rating agencies. These initiatives reflect BRICS' commitment to adopting and developing new technologies to promote economic cooperation, innovation, and security while reducing dependence on traditional financial infrastructures dominated by the West (Khachaturyan, 2024; Reuters, 2024a, 2024b).

In conclusion, the BRICS recognize that new technologies, and in particular AI, are playing an increasingly central role in international security as well. AI, in fact, provides innovative tools for cybersecurity, enhancing the ability of BRICS countries to respond to threats originating from cyberspace. In this regard, Russia, for example, has developed advanced AI-based systems to protect its critical infrastructure from cyberattacks, while China uses AI to monitor its population and prevent subversive activities, although this raises concerns about privacy and state surveillance. The adoption of advanced technologies like AI also has significant implications for maritime security. China, for instance, has strategic interests in safeguarding maritime routes across the Indian Ocean, which are crucial for international trade. AI-based maritime surveillance systems can detect anomalies and potential threats, such as piracy or illegal activities, significantly enhancing security along global trade routes and ensuring safe access to natural resources.

In the next section, we will further explore the security aspect.

International Security and the Role of the BRICS: Military Spending and Defense Cooperation

A recent study by the German Institute for Global and Area Studies in Hamburg (Valencia, 2024), highlights how the BRICS countries have significantly increased their military spending in recent years. This phenomenon is occurring alongside greater attention to modernizing armed forces and acquiring new military technologies, including drones, AI applied to defense, and cyberwarfare capabilities. Although the total military spending of the BRICS remains lower than that of NATO, it is evident that the strategic orientation of the bloc's members is increasingly focused on protecting their national sovereignties and creating autonomous military capabilities.

The BRICS group was not established as a military alliance; nonetheless, increasing cooperation in defense, arms production, and cybersecurity highlights an emerging dimension of the group's strategic posture. China and Russia, in particular, have deepened their collaboration in the defense sector through joint exercises and the exchange of advanced technologies. Prior to 2014, their cooperation was primarily economic, but the annexation of Crimea marked a turning point. Russia's isolation from Ukraine's defense industry and Western partners, made China a crucial source of technological components. In return, China gained access to advanced Russian military technologies, including missile systems, air defense platforms, and electronic warfare capabilities. Since 2017, Russia and China have conducted over 100 joint military exercises in regions such as the Mediterranean, the Arctic Circle, and off the coast of South Africa (Daly, 2025). By 2019, they formalized a "comprehensive strategic partnership," encompassing agreements on joint missile early-warning systems and detailed roadmaps for military cooperation. From 2022 onwards, China has become an essential partner for sustaining Russia's war effort in Ukraine, particularly in the defense sector. Despite international pressure from the US, the EU, and Ukraine to leverage China's influence over Moscow toward a peaceful resolution (Balazs, 2025), China has maintained a dual-track approach: refraining from direct involvement in the conflict while continuing to strengthen strategic cooperation with Russia in areas unrelated to active hostilities (Rácz & Hrytsenko, 2025; Von Essen, 2025). Some journalistic sources also suggest that the Sino-Russian strategic partnership may have implications beyond Ukraine, including potential coordination regarding Taiwan (Belton & Shepherd, 2025). Diplomatic and symbolic gestures, such as Xi Jinping's visit to Moscow in May 2024—attending a military parade in support of Putin without making explicit commitments regarding Ukraine—and Putin's reciprocal attendance at Beijing's military parade during the SCO Summit in August 2025, underscore this alignment.

The SCO further exemplifies this strategic collaboration. Originally conceived to mediate territorial disputes among member states, the SCO has progressively institutionalized, expanding cooperation in security, economic, energy, and cultural domains. Seen as China's response to US containment in the Indo-Pacific and Russia's to NATO expansion, the SCO increasingly functions as a counter-Western bloc. Its military and security agenda is guided by the shared goal of countering terrorism, extremism, and separatism, as outlined in its founding document, the Shanghai Convention on Combating Terrorism, Separatism, and Extremism. This focus reflects the primary concern of key members—particularly China and Russia—to preserve territorial status quo amid regional ethnic tensions, secessionist pressures, and external interventions. The SCO's rise has prompted the US to strengthen the Quadrilateral Security Dialogue (Quad), originally established in 2007 and revitalized in 2017, to counter China's growing influence and serve as a strategic counterweight. India's position is particularly complex: as a 2017 SCO member, it navigates relationships with China, Russia, and the West while participating in the US-led Quad and facing ongoing border tensions with China. Nevertheless, the SCO has inherent limitations. It is not a formal alliance with a unified geopolitical agenda, and member states maintain divergent strategic interests. China and Russia cooperate closely but have distinct priorities: Russia remains focused on countering NATO's presence, especially in its near abroad (Ukraine and the post-Soviet space), while China prioritizes regional ambitions in East Asia, including Taiwan, the South China Sea, and broader global influence, particularly in Africa and the Indo-Pacific (Soong, 2025). These differing objectives constrain the scope of military cooperation beyond their immediate spheres of interest, as neither state is willing to subordinate its strategic autonomy to the other. This limited trust is also reflected in joint military exercises, which serve more as demonstrations of cooperative intent to external observers than as genuine efforts to enhance interoperability between Russian and Chinese forces.

Regarding the relationship between China and India, it is characterized by a complex interplay of cooperation and competition. Both countries are emerging powers with rapidly growing economies and significant strategic interests, collaborating in various multilateral forums such as the G20, and of course the BRICS and the SCO. Within these frameworks, they promote global economic development and regional stability. Bilateral trade is also significant: China is one of India's main trading partners, although the trade balance heavily favors China, raising concerns in New Delhi. At the same time, competition remains evident (Fong, 2025). The India–China rivalry reflects both nations' ambitions to become global powers and their differing perceptions of national security. Key points of contention include disputed territories, regional influence in Asia and the Indian Ocean, relations with Pakistan, and participation in strategic initiatives such as China's Belt and Road Initiative. Territorial disputes along the Himalayan border have historically caused military tensions, while both countries seek to extend their economic and technological influence across Asia and beyond (Verma & Papa, 2021). Nonetheless, there are signs of a willingness to reduce tensions. During the 2024 BRICS Summit in Kazan, China and India reached agreements indicating a mutual interest in balance and cooperation. Indeed, China and India reached an agreement on joint patrolling of the contended Line of Actual Control areas (Hindustan Times, 2024). This rapprochement was further reflected in the cordial interactions between President Modi and Chinese leaders at the most recent SCO summit in Tianjin. However, initiatives such as China's Belt and Road projects and India's own infrastructure programs continue to serve as strategic tools for asserting regional influence. Looking ahead, the trajectory of Sino–Indian relations will depend on the ability to balance cooperation with competition. While trade and multilateral collaboration offer benefits, potential military escalation or economic tensions could undermine regional and global stability, making careful management of the inherent ambiguities in this relationship essential. The current US administration under Trump appears to indirectly encourage closer ties between China and India. If US policies continue to emphasize trade barriers and limited dialogue, the Sino-Indian partnership could strengthen as a counterbalance within the current global order.

A similar pattern can be observed with Brazil, which, facing US sanctions, seeks to diversify its strategic partnerships, including within the

BRICS framework. In the context of growing diplomatic tensions with the US, the Brazilian government has expressed its intention to enhance military cooperation, particularly with China. A symbolic step in this direction was the decision to assign generals as military attachés to the Brazilian embassy in China, a practice previously reserved for the US. For Brazil, engagement with China represents a natural evolution of an already well-established bilateral relationship in trade, finance, and technology, further strengthened within the BRICS framework. This approach serves as a strategy to diversify alliances and reduce dependence on Washington in sensitive security and defense matters. However, bilateral tensions have resurfaced due to recent developments in the Caribbean, where the US maintains an unprecedented military presence near Venezuela. The deployment of the USS Lake Erie, a guided-missile cruiser equipped with the AEGIS system, and the nuclear attack submarine USS Newport News has raised concerns in Brasília. This militarization threatens to further strain US–Latin American relations, with Brazil highlighting the risks associated with the introduction of nuclear-armed submarines in regional waters. Additionally, the cancellation of the most recent Formosa military exercise with the US has been interpreted as a signal of cooling bilateral cooperation. Overall, Brazil is navigating a complex landscape, balancing its international relations while exploring new strategic partnerships amid tensions with the US (Zona Militar, 2025). Taking advantage of this intricate situation, China is gradually expanding its influence on Latin American and Caribbean security through its Global Security Initiative (GSI), launched in 2022. Unlike traditional approaches based on military alliances or geopolitical confrontation, the Chinese strategy emphasizes internal security, law enforcement, and local governance, aiming to address gaps faced by many Latin American governments. The initiative features four key elements: it prioritizes cooperation with local law enforcement rather than central military forces; it actively engages local and regional actors beyond national governments; it proposes a holistic security model integrating technology, infrastructure, and governance; and it avoids imposing political or governance conditions, focusing instead on pragmatic and effective solutions (Fonseca et al., 2025).

Simultaneously, India and Brazil are pursuing initiatives to increase self-sufficiency in arms production, reducing reliance on Western suppliers. During President Luiz Inácio Lula da Silva's planned visit to India in 2026, both countries will likely reinforce their strategic alignment in defense and security through joint military exercises, high-level delegations, and the new Agreement on the Exchange and Mutual Protection of Classified Information. They have also launched a Bilateral Cybersecurity Dialogue to enhance cooperation and exchange perspectives on cyber threats. Defense collaboration is expanding in areas such as the C-390 Millennium aircraft and India's Akash missile system, with Embraer proposing up to 80 multi-role transport aircraft for the Indian Air Force under the Medium Transport Aircraft program and exploring joint production with Mahindra Defence. Brazil is evaluating the Akash medium-range missile for its air defense independently, while both countries continue to develop defense–industrial partnerships in small arms, munitions, helicopters, and aerospace platforms. Brazil has strengthened its institutional presence by assigning air and naval attachés to its embassy in New Delhi, signaling a deeper commitment to military and technological cooperation. Naval collaboration, including submarine operations and training under the Scorpène Club, remains another shared priority. These initiatives set the stage for further strategic engagement at the Modi–Lula summit in February 2026, where co-development, technology sharing, and trusted defense production are expected to feature prominently in their broader partnership (Siddiqui, 2025; Ministry of External Affairs Government of India, 2025).

Brazil is also expanding its security and defense cooperation with South Africa. Beyond joint military exercises, the two countries have developed a multifaceted partnership encompassing the defense industry and broader strategic collaboration. A key milestone in this relationship is the Memorandum of Understanding between Brazil's Embraer and South Africa's Denel, focusing on the KC-390 Millennium aircraft, aerostructure manufacturing, and the establishment of maintenance, repair, and overhaul capabilities in South Africa, aimed at enhancing its military airlift capacity (Defence Turkey, 2025). This partnership reflects broader South Atlantic defense priorities, as Brazil seeks to consolidate its geopolitical influence and strengthen its maritime security posture, particularly in the Gulf of Guinea (Araujo, 2024). Historical ties and evolving diplomatic–military relations between Brazil and African nations provide a solid foundation for engagement within multilateral frameworks such as the Community of Portuguese Language Countries and the Zone of Peace and Cooperation of the South Atlantic. High-level visits, including the November 6, 2024, delegation to the Lohatlha Combat Training Centre and the 44 Parachute Regiment in Bloemfontein, highlight the practical dimension of this cooperation, featuring demonstrations of parachute operations, combat engineering, riot control, fire-and-movement drills, and armored vehicle capabilities (Martin, 2024). Collectively, these initiatives underscore the strategic significance of Brazil–South Africa defense relations, emphasizing regional stability, enhanced military readiness, and the strengthening of South–South strategic partnerships.

Meanwhile, South Africa is working to strengthen its role in regional security through bilateral and multilateral agreements with other BRICS members. Indeed, in addition to the initiatives already mentioned with Brazil, there is also Exercise Ibsamar VIII, a trilateral maritime exercise involving South Africa, Brazil, and India, which highlights South Africa's ongoing efforts to deepen its defense and security relations with both countries. Hosted along South Africa's strategic coastline, the exercise provides a platform for extensive naval cooperation, combining harbor operations with complex sea-phase maneuvers. Participating forces—including South Africa's SAS Amatola, Brazil's BNS Defensora, and India's INS Talwar—engaged in a wide range of activities, such as tactical drills, search and rescue operations, and maritime security exercises, supported by helicopters and Special Forces teams. Beyond operational training, Ibsamar VIII underscores South Africa's commitment to fostering multilateral partnerships, enhancing interoperability, and building mutual trust with emerging global naval powers. Technological integration, exemplified by India's NISHAR system for real-time information sharing, further strengthens coordinated responses to shared challenges like piracy, illegal fishing, and drug trafficking. Overall, Exercise Ibsamar VIII reflects South Africa's strategic intention to cultivate robust defense ties with Brazil and India, contributing to regional maritime security and reinforcing South–South cooperation.

With China, South Africa has actively sought to strengthen military and security cooperation, framing their partnership as a joint stance against perceived external "bullying and hegemony." This strategic alignment has gained particular significance in light of recent tensions between Pretoria and Washington, stemming from South Africa's post-apartheid land restitution policies and the Trump administration's designation of a small group of Afrikaners as refugees (China-Global South Project, 2025). The formal framework for Sino-South African defense cooperation was established in 2000 with the Pretoria Declaration, with the first official meeting of the China–South Africa Defense Committee held in 2003. Since then, bilateral military relations have deepened, encompassing the training of South African military personnel in China, the provision of advanced electronic equipment to South African armed forces, and enhanced intelligence and strategic coordination. Naval exercises, such as the trilateral *Mosi Exercise* involving China, Russia, and South Africa, have further consolidated this military partnership, underscoring Pretoria's growing willingness to engage with non-Western security actors and signaling a broader shift in both regional and global power dynamics (Martin, 2025).

In addition to its strategic relations with China, Russia has been actively strengthening military and defense ties with South Africa. In 2024, the two countries signed an agreement to enhance bilateral military cooperation, and they have conducted joint military exercises to consolidate their partnership. During a meeting, General Oleg Salyukov, Commander of the Russian Ground Forces, emphasized that Russia views collaboration with African partners as strategic and long-term, describing its relations with South Africa as friendly, reliable, and equitable (Guliyeva, 2024). This development occurs within a broader framework of increasing trilateral cooperation among Russia, South Africa, and China, which has included joint naval exercises in the Indian Ocean (South African Government, 2025). While such exercises have raised concerns among Western nations, the governments involved have characterized them as routine activities between sovereign states. Furthermore, Russia and South Africa are developing joint defense manufacturing projects for both domestic armed forces and third-party countries, including the establishment of a helicopter maintenance center in southern Africa. This deepening military cooperation reflects a wider strategic alignment, with Pretoria reaffirming its support for Moscow and resisting pressure from NATO countries to curtail bilateral ties.

Similarly, Russia has been consolidating its defense relationship with Brazil, shaped by the current international context marked by Western sanctions against Moscow and the US' protectionist policies under the Trump administration, which have negatively affected several countries, including Brazil (as previously mentioned). In May 2025, Brazilian President Luiz Inácio Lula da Silva visited Moscow—the first such visit in fifteen years—and proposed a "strategic partnership" between Brazil and Russia. The Kremlin meeting emphasized collaboration in key areas such as nuclear energy, defense, space, science, technology, education, and research, with a particular focus on the development of Russian small modular reactors, formalized through bilateral memoranda. Lula also criticized US global tariff policies for undermining free trade and multilateralism. Putin, in turn, highlighted Brazil's role as a major food supplier and underscored Russia's significance as an exporter of oil and fertilizers to the Brazilian market. The visit took place against the backdrop of the ongoing Russia–Ukraine conflict, during which Lula sought to position Brazil as a mediator promoting negotiated peace, while maintaining a controversial stance regarding the responsibilities of the parties involved (The Moscow Times, 2025).

Russia's defense and military ties with India represent another pillar of its strategic outreach. India and Russia have long maintained a robust partnership characterized by joint production, technology transfer, and major arms procurement, including projects such as the BrahMos supersonic cruise missile and the AK-203 rifle. Cooperation extends to the operation of Russian aircraft carriers like the INS Vikramaditya and the delivery of S-400 air defense systems. Over time, the relationship has evolved from a buyer-seller dynamic to encompass joint research and development, despite shifting geopolitical pressures and Western influence. In August 2025, India and Russia discussed ways to further intensify their defense collaboration and reaffirmed the importance of expanding cooperation in areas such as energy, economy, and diplomacy to promote sustainable growth and address shared global challenges (DD News, 2025). India's foreign policy is often described as a "dual alignment," balancing relations with both Russia and the US. Historically non-aligned, India has maintained a flexible foreign policy, leveraging its strategic position to extract concessions from major powers and shape regional security architecture to its advantage. Its sustained defense cooperation with Russia, including discounted oil imports, reflects both strategic necessity and energy dependency, reinforcing partnerships exemplified by the S-400 systems and the BrahMos project. In the context of growing US sanctions and geopolitical tensions, these ties may be further strengthened in the coming years, mirroring dynamics observed in Brazil (Kaura, 2025).

The Role of the BRICS in Global Security

One of the main and recurring claims made by the BRICS during their summits is their commitment to contributing to a safer world and to playing a greater role in the governance of global security (Slonskaya, 2024). Although the conflict between Russia and Ukraine is still ongoing, and tensions between China and the US over Taiwan remain high, it is important to note that—unlike the US, which has played the role of global leader for nearly a century—these "rising states," often accused of destabilizing the world order, have historically been far less aggressive (Chan & Hu, 2025). In contrast, the US has repeatedly used its military power to promote its own vision of the world (Chan & Hu, 2025). Therefore, despite some undeniable contradictions, it is fair to argue that the BRICS' commitment to building a safer global order will become increasingly necessary in the future. In this sense, a key issue of international security addressed by the BRICS is the fight against terrorism. Although the members of the bloc have different approaches to the problem—China, for example, has a strict policy against separatism and terrorism, while India emphasizes the need for regional cooperation—the agreement on the principles of international cooperation in the fight against terrorism is common ground. Furthermore, the BRICS are working to develop stronger cooperation in the management of international crises, with particular focus on conflict prevention and cybersecurity management.

As is well known, the end of the Cold War marked the beginning of a period of profound transformation in the international system. The bipolar order dominated by the US and the Soviet Union dissolved, giving way to Washington's attempt to establish a unipolar order shaped around its own national interests. However, this hegemony proved to be short-lived. The rapid rise of emerging economies made it increasingly untenable to sustain an international balance centered on a single pole of power, paving the way for a more multipolar world order. Within this evolving context, the BRICS group emerged, united by the shared ambition to redefine the rules of global governance and to assert a stronger collective voice in international affairs. Despite numerous criticisms and pessimistic forecasts—particularly from Western analysts—the BRICS have not only endured but have gradually expanded their agenda. Initially focused primarily on economic and trade-related issues, the group has progressively broadened its scope to include key global challenges such as international security, terrorism, nuclear proliferation, territorial disputes, organized and cybercrime, poverty, demographic pressures, and climate change, as we have seen in the chapters of this book. This evolution reflects a growing awareness that the postwar international security system is no longer adequate to address the complexities of the contemporary world. While the BRICS recognize the central role of the United Nations in promoting international peace and security, they consistently stress the need for a deep reform of its institutions—most notably, the Security Council. The current composition of this body fails to reflect the power dynamics of the twenty-first century. Countries such as India, Brazil, and South Africa, which aspire to a more prominent role in global governance, have called for permanent membership, while Russia and China—already permanent members—support the need for reform. Yet, the difficulty of reaching consensus, particularly regarding the sensitive issue of the veto power, has so far hindered meaningful progress. Nevertheless, the urgency of reforming the UN Security Council stems not only from questions of legitimacy and representativeness but also from the anachronistic nature of its current structure. The world order has changed dramatically since 1945: approximately 70% of contemporary international crises occur in Africa and Asia—regions that, excluding China, have no permanent representation on the Council (Petrone, 2021).

Thus, a key question for the near future of global security concerns whether and how the UN will undergo reform, and whether such reform will truly reflect today's multipolar composition rather than the preferences of a few dominant actors. This issue has become increasingly pressing, especially following US President Donald Trump's speech at the UN General Assembly on September 23, 2025, in which he harshly criticized the organization and sought to highlight its weaknesses (United Nations, 2025). Such statements risk undermining multilateralism and could negatively affect the evolution of global policies in the years ahead. Despite its structural limitations, largely due to an outdated institutional design, the UN remains a vital organ of global governance. It therefore requires a renewed vision, which necessarily entails a reform process—beginning with the Security Council. In practice, China and Russia may be reluctant to expand the Council, particularly if enlargement implies extending veto power to new members such as India, with whom China maintains longstanding rivalries. Nevertheless, the very existence of the BRICS grouping, along with its ongoing expansion and deepening cooperation, is likely to stimulate more concrete and serious discussions on the need to reform the UN Security Council in the coming years.

The BRICS also play an active role in UN peacekeeping operations, contributing troops, resources, and expertise. However, they maintain a cautious stance toward the "Responsibility to Protect" (R2P) doctrine, concerned that it could serve as a pretext for unilateral interventions or infringements on national sovereignty—often justified under the guise of humanitarian missions. Consequently, the BRICS emphasize the peaceful resolution of crises through dialogue and diplomacy, rejecting the use of force except as a last resort and always in full respect of international law

(Slonskaya, 2024). Within this framework, the internal diversity of the group constitutes both a challenge and an opportunity. The five BRICS countries represent ancient civilizations, distinct cultural traditions, and sometimes divergent geopolitical interests—as evidenced by tensions between India and China, or the differing global ambitions of Russia, China, Brazil, and India. Yet, this heterogeneity can also generate a beneficial complementarity: China contributes industrial capacity and labor; Russia provides natural resources; India offers technological and digital expertise; while Brazil and South Africa supply investment opportunities and connections to Latin American and African markets. This interdependence helps mitigate conflict risks and fosters cooperation based on shared and mutually reinforcing interests (Slonskaya, 2024).

Although the BRICS do not constitute an integrative bloc comparable to the EU, they function as a platform for coordination among emerging economies that share the ambition to reform the global order and to advance alternative models of development and governance. The group's critique of the current Western-centric international order does not imply an anti-Western posture; rather, it reflects an effort to construct a more balanced, inclusive, and multipolar system. Today, the BRICS represent a major actor in global security and governance. Their growing economic weight, political assertiveness, and commitment to collective action make them an increasingly influential force in international decision-making. The group's success will depend on its capacity to overcome internal rivalries, maintain a unified approach, and translate political declarations into concrete action. Only by doing so can the BRICS establish themselves as a driving force for the transformation of the world order and as promoters of a new vision of international security and cooperation. A positive example of this growing institutionalization is the group's first joint declaration on nuclear energy. On September 26, 2025, the annual conference of the BRICS Nuclear Energy Platform was held in Moscow as part of the World Atomic Week (WAW-2025). The meeting reviewed the results achieved in 2025, outlined prospects for 2026, and approved the Platform's first strategic document. This document identifies priority areas of cooperation—ranging from human resource development and financing to supply chain sustainability, reactor construction, fuel-cycle technologies, and the promotion of public acceptance of nuclear energy—and sets out guidelines for organizational growth. Currently, the BRICS account for roughly one-third of all operational nuclear power plants and over 70% of those under construction. They are expected to represent at least two-thirds of new global nuclear capacity by 2030. The establishment and consolidation of the BRICS Nuclear Energy Platform signal the group's intention to play a decisive role in shaping the future of global energy. More broadly, this initiative represents a step toward greater institutionalization of the BRICS within the global energy landscape and a means of balancing the influence of Western-dominated nuclear institutions. It also illustrates the group's pursuit of greater autonomy and a distinct vision of security less dependent on Western paradigms (Atom Media, 2025).

Additional examples include the group's engagement with emerging technologies and artificial intelligence, and their commitment to developing a new global security governance framework. In this regard, during a meeting held in Brasília in May 2025, the national security advisors of BRICS countries reaffirmed their shared commitments to global cooperation, a multipolar order, and the peaceful resolution of conflicts. Under Brazil's presidency, discussions focused on pressing security challenges such as armed conflicts and humanitarian crises, and emphasized the need to strengthen multilateral mechanisms rather than resort to unilateral action. The BRICS also reiterated their determination to play an active role in conflict mediation—not merely as passive observers, but as proactive actors capable of proposing peaceful solutions. They reaffirmed their support for international law, multilateral institutions, and the rejection of any unipolar dominance. Specific issues discussed included the conflicts in Ukraine and the Middle East, with renewed calls for ceasefires, unimpeded humanitarian access, and the "multilateralization" of peace initiatives whenever appropriate (BRICS, 2025c; Ministry of Foreign Affairs of the People's Republic of China, 2025).

Thus, taken together, these positions demonstrate that the BRICS envision a diplomatic, dialogue-based approach to global security—one rooted in multipolarism and multilateral cooperation, and in clear opposition to the resurgence of unilateralism that some US policies appear to encourage.

NATO-BRICS Relations: Strategic Competition and Emerging Tensions

Relations between NATO and the BRICS are characterized by complexity, strategic competition, and growing geopolitical tensions. NATO increasingly perceives Russia and China as systemic challenges, particularly given their ambitions to reshape the global order and promote alternative governance models. Yet, the picture is not uniformly adversarial. Some BRICS members—such as India—have historically maintained cooperative relations with Western countries on selected issues, including nuclear non-proliferation, counterterrorism, and the fight against transnational organized crime. This pragmatic engagement, however, has been periodically strained, for example following the imposition of tariffs by the US on Indian goods. Another emblematic case is Turkey: although a longstanding NATO member, it has formally expressed interest in joining the BRICS framework, underscoring the fluidity and complexity of current alignments (The New Arab Staff, 2024).

Despite these nuances, a fundamental distinction must be made between the two groupings. NATO was established as a military alliance under a collective defense framework, whereas the BRICS is not a military bloc but rather a coalition focused on economic, political, and developmental cooperation. Nonetheless, the recent expansion of the group into BRICS Plus could be perceived by Western actors as a potential strategic challenge, particularly as it broadens the group's influence across multiple regions and sectors.

A recurring theme in BRICS rhetoric is the invocation of the legacy of the Non-Aligned Movement (NAM), founded in Belgrade in 1961. Like the NAM, the BRICS present themselves as advocates of multipolarity and autonomy from dominant blocs—neither aligned with the US-led Western alliance (represented militarily by NATO) nor with any rival military coalition. However, the post–Cold War dissolution of the Warsaw Pact, juxtaposed with NATO's continued expansion and activity, complicates direct analogies. Leaders such as Brazilian President Luiz Inácio Lula da Silva have suggested that the BRICS embody the spirit of non-alignment (Mišković, 2025), yet current realities—particularly Russia's confrontation with NATO-backed Ukraine—introduce profound asymmetries and contradictions within the group. Since 2022, Russia's war in Ukraine has intensified hostilities with NATO members, many of which have provided substantial military and logistical support to Kyiv. Recent developments, including the US administration's increased pressure on NATO allies to raise defense spending and threats of deploying advanced weaponry to support Ukraine, have further escalated tensions. The re-election of President Donald Trump appears to have added uncertainty: while his meeting with Russian President Vladimir Putin in Alaska (in August 2025) suggested a willingness to negotiate an end to the conflict, subsequent statements and actions—especially in the final months of 2025—indicate a shift toward an undefined stance. Indeed, President Trump initially appeared to adopt a more confrontational posture, then a milder one, only to return once again to more threatening rhetoric, and shortly thereafter to appear more conciliatory again, as the twenty-eight-point peace proposal he advanced in November 2025 seems to demonstrate, at least at the time of writing this book. In any case, this suggests a policy driven more by mood than by coherent strategy. Alternatively, these fluctuations in attitude might reflect a certain underlying strategy—one that, however, remains difficult to discern. In any case, a renewed push for military spending among NATO members, raises the risk of a broader and potentially catastrophic escalation.

Beyond the immediate conflict with Russia, NATO's strategic evolution reveals a notable expansion of its scope beyond traditional defense. In response to new global challenges and perceived threats, the Alliance has progressively incorporated non-military dimensions into its agenda, including cyber defense, energy infrastructure protection, supply chain resilience, and space security (Anis, 2025). This diversification of NATO's operational domains suggests not only an adaptation to contemporary security concerns but also, indirectly, a coordinated effort to counterbalance the growing influence of the BRICS and their expanding areas of cooperation, such as technology, infrastructure, and financial governance. From a diplomatic standpoint, one possible strategy for NATO and its leading members, particularly the US, could involve pursuing a policy of "decoupling" BRICS members by fostering bilateral engagements aimed at weakening intra-group cohesion. Such a strategy, if successful, might constrain China's global ambitions by isolating it from other emerging powers. However, given President Trump's often unilateral and confrontational approach to foreign policy, the opposite effect could occur: heightened US pressure may instead drive BRICS countries closer together, reinforcing their collective resolve to challenge Western dominance. Indeed, the BRICS are already advancing several initiatives designed to enhance autonomy and resilience vis-à-vis Western institutions. These include the aforementioned efforts toward de-dollarization, the establishment of alternative financial architectures such as the NDB, joint technological and AI collaborations, and even defense cooperation through joint exercises, memoranda of understanding, and strategic agreements. Should Western policies become increasingly coercive, a plausible future scenario could involve the formalization of deeper security or even military arrangements among BRICS Plus members—an outcome that would risk ushering in a new Cold War dynamic, with unpredictable and potentially severe consequences for global stability.

In summary, the evolving relationship between NATO and the BRICS reflects broader shifts in the international order. The intersection of technological innovation, security realignments, and competing visions of global governance highlights the centrality of the BRICS in shaping future geopolitical trajectories. While internal divergences persist, the group's growing cooperation in strategic sectors, advocacy for institutional reform, and collective ambition to reduce dependence on Western powers position the BRICS as a decisive actor in the transformation of the twenty-first-century global order.

References

Aguirre Ernst, M. (2025, August 15). Trump is attacking Brazil to weaken BRICS – but his plan might backfire. *Chatham House*. https://www.chathamhouse.org/2025/08/trump-attacking-brazil-weaken-brics-his-plan-might-backfire

AI CERTS. (2025, March 09). India's ambitious AI Mission: Government launches strategic portals to accelerate artificial intelligence development. https://news.aicerts.ai/news/indias-ambitious-ai-mission-government-launches-strategic-portals-to-accelerate-artificial-intelligence-development/

Anis, K. (2025, July 11). BRICS vs NATO: Economic alliances redefining power blocks. *DXB News Network*. https://www.dxbnewsnetwork.com/brics-vs-nato-economic-alliances-redefining-power-blocks

Araujo, L. E. d. (2024). Strengthening ties: Brazil's defense strategy in the South Atlantic through African alliances. *Revista Delos, 17*(61), 1–17. https://doi.org/10.55905/rdelosv17.n61-166

Atom Media. (2025, September 26). The BRICS Nuclear Energy Platform conference was held as part of the World Atomic Week (WAW). https://atommedia.online/en/press-releases/na-vsemirnoy-atomnoy-nedele-waw-sostoyalas-itogovaya-konferentsiya-platformy-briks-po-atomnoy-energe/

Balazs, D. (2025, May 9). The duality in China's security relations with Russia. *The Diplomat*. https://thediplomat.com/2025/05/the-duality-in-chinas-security-relations-with-russia/

Baschuk, B. (2023, August 23). How global trade changes with BRICS on the rise. *Bloomberg*. https://www.bloomberg.com/news/newsletters/2023-08-23/supply-chain-latest-how-global-trade-changes-with-saudi-indonesia-in-brics

BBC News. (2025, October 26). Will Trump's new rare-earth deals mark turning point in rivalry with China? BBC News. https://www.bbc.com/news/articles/cj6ny24j0r3o

Belton, C. & Shepherd, C. (2025, September 26). Russia is helping prepare China to attack Taiwan, documents suggest. *The Washington Post*. https://www.washingtonpost.com/world/2025/09/26/russia-china-weapons-sales-air-assault/

BRICS. (2015). Memorandum of understanding on cooperation in science, technology, and innovation. https://www.brics.utoronto.ca/docs/BRICS%20STI%20MoU%20ENGLISH.pdf

BRICS Leaders Meeting. (2025a, July 6). 17th BRICS Summit: Rio de Janeiro Declaration. http://www.brics.utoronto.ca/docs/250706-declaration.html

BRICS. (2025b, April 11). Artificial Intelligence Governance in BRICS: Cooperation and Development for Social Inclusion. https://brics.br/en/news/articles/artificial-intelligence-governance-in-brics-cooperation-and-development-for-social-inclusion

BRICS. (2025c, May 1). BRICS aligns positions and commitments on multilateralism, global peace, and tech security. https://brics.br/en/news/brics-aligns-positions-and-commitments-on-multilateralism-global-peace-and-tech-security

BRICS Leaders Meeting. (2024, October 23). 16th BRICS Summit: Kazan Declaration. https://cdn.brics-russia2024.ru/upload/docs/Kazan_Declaration_FINAL.pdf?1729693488349783

BRICS Plus Universities Association. (n.d.). Retrieved October 28, 2025, from https://brics.world/.

Bryanski, G. (2024, December 11). Russia teams up with BRICS to create AI alliance, Putin says. *Reuters*. https://www.reuters.com/technology/artificial-intelligence/russia-teams-up-with-brics-create-ai-alliance-putin-says-2024-12-11/

CADE Project. (2025, July 7). BRICS leaders agree on joint approach to technology, finance, and global challenges. https://cadeproject.org/updates/brics-leaders-agree-on-joint-approach-to-technology-finance-and-global-challenges/

Chan, S., & Hu, W. (2025). Rising states and evolving global governance: the case of China. *International Affairs, 101*(2), 381–397. https://doi.org/10.1093/ia/iiae330

China Association for Science and Technology. (2025, January 10). The China-BRICS artificial intelligence development and cooperation center's operational base inaugurated in Shanghai. https://voc-gj.cast.org.cn/index/info?api=GwArticle&id=33870

China-Global South Project. (2025, June 11). Chinese defense minister calls for closer cooperation with South Africa. https://chinaglobalsouth.com/2025/06/11/china-south-africa-military-ties/

Council on Foreign Relations. (2021). Assessing China's digital silk road initiative a transformative approach to technology financing or a danger to freedoms?. https://www.cfr.org/china-digital-silk-road/

Cyman, D., Gromova, E., & Juchnevicius, E. (2021). Regulation of Artificial Intelligence in BRICS and the European Union. *BRICS Law Journal, 8*(1), 86–115. https://doi.org/10.21684/2412-2343-2021-8-1-86-115

Daly, R. (2025, July 8). China and Russia: Quietly going steady?. *Wilson Center.* https://www.wilsoncenter.org/blog-post/china-and-russia-quietly-going-steady

DD News. (2025, August 6). India and Russia discuss ways to further intensify defence partnership. https://ddnews.gov.in/en/india-and-russia-discuss-ways-to-further-intensify-defence-partnership/

De Guzman, C. & Schneid, R. (2025, May 23). Why South Africa is torn over the Trump-Ramaphosa showdown. *TIME.* https://time.com/7288363/south-africa-reacts-trump-ramaphosa-oval-office/

Defence Turkey. (2025, May). Embraer and Denel sign MoU to cooperate on the KC-390 Millennium. *Defence Turkey Magazine*, Issue 139. https://www.defenceturkey.com/en/content/embraer-and-denel-sign-mou-to-cooperate-on-the-kc-390-millennium-6272

Dezhina, I. (2024). Russia and the new BRICS countries: Potentials and limitations of scientific and technological cooperation. *Russie.Eurasie.Visions*, No. 136, Ifri, September.

Falk, F. (2025, August 27). Saudi Arabia's AI strategy 2030 is more radical than you think. *Beam.ai.* https://beam.ai/agentic-insights/saudi-arabias-ai-strategy-2030-is-more-radical-than-you-think.

Fauchoux, V. & Perissinotto, J. (2023, November 9). Artificial intelligence: Joe Biden's executive order vs. the European AI Act – Common Goals?. *DDG.* https://www.ddg.fr/actualite/ai-joe-bidens-executive-order-vs-the-european-ai-act-common-goals.

Fong, C. (2025, September 10). The China-India relationship: Between cooperation and competition. *Council on Foreign Relations.* https://www.cfr.org/backgrounder/china-india-relationship-between-cooperation-and-competition

Fonseca, B., Writt, N., & Brown, M. (2025, September 11). China's quiet security push in Latin America. *Americas Quarterly.* https://www.americasquarterly.org/article/chinas-quiet-security-push/.

Gavin, M. (2025, May 21). The tensions behind the Trump-Ramaphosa White House meeting. *Council on Foreign Relations.* https://www.cfr.org/blog/tensions-behind-trump-ramaphosa-white-house-meeting

Geohistory. (2022). Artificial intelligence in Russia. https://geohistory.today/artificial-intelligence-in-russia/.
Goswami, A. (2024). The role of artificial intelligence in fostering multifaceted cooperation among BRICS nations. African Policy Research Institute. https://afripoli.org/the-role-of-artificial-intelligence-in-fostering-multifaceted-cooperation-among-brics-nations
Guliyeva, V. (2024, October 28). Russia, South Africa strengthen military cooperation. *Caliber.Az*. https://caliber.az/en/post/russia-south-africa-strengthen-military-cooperation
Gumede, L. (2024). How South Africa can leverage the artificial intelligence revolution. *The Inclusive Society Institute* (ISI). https://www.inclusivesociety.org.za/post/how-south-africa-can-leverage-the-artificial-intelligence-revolution#:~:text=South%20Africa's%20Current%20AI%20Strategy,research%20at%20South%20African%20Universities
Haski, P. (2017, November 20). La geopolitica dell'intelligenza artificiale. *Internazionale*. https://www.internazionale.it/opinione/pierre-haski/2017/09/20/intelligenza-artificiale-geopolitica
Hindustan Times. (2024). India-China relations have progressed: S Jaishankar in Lok Sabha. https://www.hindustantimes.com/india-news/indiachina-relations-have-progressed-s-jaishankar-in-lok-sabha-101733216118721.html
International Cooperation Division. (2015, March 18). BRICS memorandum of understanding on cooperation in the field of science, technology and innovation. Department of Science & Technology, Government of India. https://aistic.gov.in/ASEAN/imrcBRICS
Jelinek, T. (2024, April 15). AI governance: EU and US converge on risk-based approach amid stark differences. *Hertie School*. https://www.hertie-school.org/en/content/detail/content/ai-governance-eu-and-us-converge-on-risk-based-approach-amid-stark-differences
Jiang, M., & Belli, L. (2024). *Digital sovereignty with the BRICS countries: How the Global South and emerging power alliances are reshaping digital governance*. Cambridge University Press.
Kaura, V. (2025, July 21). India's diplomacy of dual alignments: Russia and the US. Royal United Services Institute. https://www.rusi.org/explore-our-research/publications/commentary/indias-diplomacy-dual-alignments-russia-and-us
Khachaturyan, M. (2024, May 3). BRICS technology and AI boom: Shaping the future of emerging economies. *TV BRICS*. https://tvbrics.com/en/news/brics-technology-and-ai-boom-shaping-the-future-of-emerging-economies/
Kwet, M. (2019). Digital colonialism: US empire and the new imperialism in the Global South. *Race & Class*. https://doi.org/10.1177/0306396818823172
Mahrenbach, L., & Papa, M. (2024, March 27). BRICS wants to shape global AI governance, too. *Fletcher Russia and Eurasia Program*. https://sites.tufts.edu/fletcherrussia/brics-wants-to-shape-global-ai-governance-too/

Martin, G. (2024, November 11). Brazilian Army Chief visits South Africa. *DefenceWeb.* https://defenceweb.co.za/land/land-land/brazilian-army-chief-visits-south-africa/

Martin, G. (2025, June 17). Sino/South African military co-operation to expand. *DefenceWeb.* https://defenceweb.co.za/joint/diplomacy-a-peace/sino-south-african-military-co-operation-to-expand/

Mehta, M. (2025, September 29). From allies to ambiguity: Quad awaits Trump's next move. *Daily Sabah.* https://www.dailysabah.com/opinion/op-ed/from-allies-to-ambiguity-quad-awaits-trumps-next-move

Meinhardt, C., Zhang, D., King, J., Haupt, A., & Cryst, E. (2025, July 24). Inside Trump's ambitious AI action plan. *Stanford Institute for Human-Centered AI.* https://hai.stanford.edu/news/inside-trumps-ambitious-ai-action-plan

Ministério da Ciência, Tecnologia e Inovações. (2024). Plano Brasileiro de Inteligência Artificial (PBIA) 2024–2028. https://www.gov.br/lncc/pt-br/assuntos/noticias/ultimas-noticias-1/plano-brasileiro-de-inteligencia-artificial-pbia-2024-2028

Ministry of External Affairs Government of India. (2025, July 8). India and Brazil – Two great nations with shared vision. https://www.mea.gov.in/bilateral-documents.htm?dtl/39783

Ministry of Foreign Affairs of the People's Republic of China. (2025, May 1). The Meeting of BRICS National Security Advisers and High Representatives on National Security Held in Brasilia. https://www.fmprc.gov.cn/eng/wjb/zzjg_663340/ggjjs_665228/xwlb_665230/202505/t20250505_11615533.html

Mišković, N. (2025, September 22). BRICS and the legacy of the Non-Aligned Movement. *Swissinfo.* https://www.swissinfo.ch/eng/war-peace/brics-and-the-legacy-of-the-non-aligned-movement/90043375

Nanda, P. (2025, September 6). Is Trump KILLING the QUAD? How new American policies could derail US-India-Japan-Australia pact?. *EurAsian Times.* https://www.eurasiantimes.com/is-trump-killing-the-quad/

Pessarlay, W. (2025, July 9). China expands AI partnerships with Brazil, Australia. *CoinGeek.* https://coingeek.com/china-expands-ai-partnerships-with-brazil-australia/

Petrone, F. (2021). BRICS and global governance: Will the grouping be able to reform the United Nations Security Council? *International Studies, 58*(3), 363–379. https://doi.org/10.1177/00208817211029409

Rácz, A. & Hrytsenko, A. (2025, June 16). Partnership short of alliance: Military cooperation between Russia and China. *Center for European Policy Analysis.* https://cepa.org/comprehensive-reports/partnership-short-of-alliance-military-cooperation-between-russia-and-china/

Reuters. (2024a, October 16). What proposals will Russia push at the BRICS summit? https://www.reuters.com/world/what-proposals-will-russia-push-brics-summit-2024-10-16/

Reuters. (2024b, October 2023). Brazil's Lula urges BRICS to create alternative payment methods. https://www.reuters.com/technology/brazils-lula-urges-brics-create-alternative-payment-methods-2024-10-23/

Rosano, R. (2024). Digital Silk Road: come la Cina aspira a diventare una superpotenza tecnologica. *MicroMega*. https://www.micromega.net/digital-silk-road-come-la-cina-aspira-a-diventare-una-superpotenza-tecnologica

Siddiqui, H. (2025, October 5). Brazil's Defence Minister visits India to boost defence ties. *Bharat Shakti*. https://bharatshakti.in/brazils-defence-minister-visits-india-to-boost-defence-ties/

Slonskaya, M. (2024). The role of BRICS in global security. MGIMO-University. https://mgimo.ru/upload/2015/10/The_Role_of_BRICS_in_Global_Security.pdf?

Soliman, M. (2025, June 5). Saudi Arabia's AI ambition, and what it means for the United States. Middle East Institute. https://www.mei.edu/publications/saudi-arabias-ai-ambition-and-what-it-means-united-states

Soong, C. (2025, July 31). China and Russia are using the Shanghai Cooperation Organization to push alternative global order. *MERICS*. https://merics.org/en/comment/china-and-russia-are-using-shanghai-cooperation-organization-push-alternative-global-order

South African Government. (2025, September 4). Defence on joint BRICS military exercise. https://www.gov.za/news/media-statements/defence-joint-brics-military-exercise-04-sep-2025

Sukhankin, S. (2025). Russia capitalizes on development of artificial intelligence in its military strategy. Eurasia Daily Monitor, 22(1). https://jamestown.org/program/russia-capitalizes-on-development-of-artificial-intelligence-in-its-military-strategy/

The Moscow Times. (2025, May 9). Brazil's Lula pitches 'strategic partnership' with Russia. https://www.themoscowtimes.com/2025/05/09/brazils-lula-pitches-strategic-partnership-with-russia-a89034

The New Arab Staff. (2024, September 3). NATO member Turkey submits formal bid to join BRICS. *The New Arab*. https://www.newarab.com/news/nato-member-turkey-submits-formal-bid-join-brics

The White House. (2025, July 7). America's AI action plan. https://www.whitehouse.gov/wp-content/uploads/2025/07/Americas-AI-Action-Plan.pdf.

Think BRICS. (2025, August 29). BRICS AI revolution - The untold story. https://thinkbrics.substack.com/p/inside-brics-push-for-ai-independence

U.S. Geological Survey. (2025). Mineral commodity summaries 2025 (ver. 1.2, March 2025): U.S. Geological Survey, p. 212. https://doi.org/10.3133/mcs2025

United Nations. (2025, September 23). US President Trump criticizes UN, NATO and climate 'hoax'. *UN News*. https://news.un.org/en/story/2025/09/1165924

Valencia, E. (2024). BRICS, BRICS plus, and the G7: a look at global military expenditure. *GIGA*. https://www.giga-hamburg.de/en/publications/contributions/brics-brics-plus-and-the-g7-a-look-at-global-military-expenditure

Verma, R., & Papa, M. (2021). BRICS amidst India-China rivalry. *Global Policy Journal*, *12*(4) https://www.globalpolicyjournal.com/articles/global-governance/brics-amidst-india-china-rivalry

Von Essen, H. (2025, May 7). Joint military exercises signal deepening Russia-China strategic alignment. *MERICS*. https://merics.org/en/comment/joint-military-exercises-signal-deepening-russia-china-strategic-alignment

Xinghui, K. (2025, October 26). US, China talks sketch out rare earths, tariff pause for Trump and Xi to consider. *Reuters*. https://www.reuters.com/world/china/ustr-greer-says-trade-talks-with-china-moving-toward-agreement-leaders-review-2025-10-26/

Xinyi, X. (2024, September 11). Emerging tech progress in BRICS promotes devt for Global South. *Global Times*. https://www.globaltimes.cn/page/202409/1319676.shtml

Zona Militar. (2025, September 11). Brazil once again challenges the U.S. by exploring options to expand military cooperation with China. *Zona Militar*. https://www.zona-militar.com/en/2025/09/11/brazil-once-again-challenges-the-u-s-by-exploring-options-to-expand-military-cooperation-with-china/

CHAPTER 8

Final Remarks

Abstract The final remarks highlight how the contemporary international system, marked by the erosion of the liberal international order and the emergence of alternative centers of power, is undergoing a profound transformation. Within this context, the BRICS coalition has become a central expression of the call for greater inclusion, equity, and pluralism in global governance. Through initiatives aimed at reforming multilateral institutions and promoting sustainable development, climate cooperation, and technological exchange, the BRICS represent both a critique of Western-centered governance and an aspiration for a more representative and balanced international order. The enlargement to the "BRICS Plus" framework further reflects their growing attractiveness among emerging economies seeking stronger global visibility. However, this transformative promise coexists with deep internal challenges. Structural asymmetries—especially China's economic predominance—along with strategic rivalries and divergent governance models threaten the group's cohesion. Climate policies remain fragmented, and institutional reform efforts have produced limited outcomes. These tensions risk turning the coalition into a pragmatic but incoherent actor rather than a unified force for systemic change. The future of the BRICS will therefore depend on their capacity to institutionalize cooperation, ensure transparency, and advance inclusive development goals. Their evolution will decisively influence whether

F. Petrone, *The BRICS and the Transformation of Global Power*,
https://doi.org/10.1007/978-3-032-23540-4_8

global governance moves toward plural cooperation or renewed fragmentation.

Keywords Global governance • Liberal International Order (LIO) • BRICS • Global South • World order • Multilateralism

The world is undergoing an epochal transition. The traditional architecture of global governance, which for decades has shaped the international system, is facing an unprecedented crisis. As this study has demonstrated, the origins of this transformation are both internal and external. Internally, the LIO is increasingly unable to respond to contemporary global challenges or to maintain the legitimacy it once enjoyed. Externally, the rise of emerging powers has profoundly altered the balance of global influence. These actors now demand, with growing assertiveness and legitimacy, a voice commensurate with their economic and diplomatic capacities. Among these forces, the BRICS coalition stands as one of the most visible manifestations of this systemic shift. By presenting themselves as advocates of a more inclusive, equitable, and plural international order, the BRICS challenge the historical dominance of Western-centric models and call for a governance system that places at its core the urgent needs of the Global South—ranging from climate change adaptation and sustainable development to technological cooperation and greater participation in international institutions. The evolution of the group from its original five members toward the "BRICS Plus" format underscores the growing appeal of this platform. Many states from the Global South view it as a promising space where their concerns are more accurately represented than within the declining structures of the liberal order.

However, the transformative potential of the BRICS is accompanied by significant contradictions and internal limitations. Despite their rhetoric of solidarity and inclusiveness, the group faces persistent divergences in strategic priorities and governance approaches. In the field of climate governance, for instance, common positions remain fragmented and often subordinated to national interests. Similarly, while the BRICS collectively advocate for reform of the UN Security Council to reflect contemporary multipolar realities, China and Russia—permanent members with veto powers—have not taken substantive steps to translate such demands into concrete institutional change. Intra-group rivalries, such as those between China and India, further complicate the cohesion of the bloc, while

China's overwhelming economic weight risks fostering perceptions of asymmetry and potential hegemony. The expansion under the BRICS Plus initiative, although symbolically significant, could exacerbate these tensions by adding new members with divergent priorities and heterogeneous governance models. The result may be a group that struggles to articulate coherent positions or to act collectively in multilateral fora. The BRICS thus embody both the promise of a transformative force in international relations and the risk of fragmentation, which could undermine their capacity to advance a credible alternative to the current order.

At the same time, Western powers are grappling with their own crises—economic stagnation, political polarization, and institutional fatigue. Yet rather than engaging constructively with emerging actors, the response has often relied on coercive instruments, unilateralism, and renewed militarization. US tariff policies, the EU's inconsistent approach to climate governance, and a general return to arms competition all reflect a tendency to preserve the status quo through power politics rather than through dialogue and reform.

The Global South, meanwhile, finds itself in a position of uncertainty. While its aspirations for greater representation are legitimate, it often struggles to find consistent support within Western frameworks. Although the BRICS give voice to its demands, they are sometimes perceived as new centers of domination rather than genuine partners in equitable development.

In this period of global interregnum—an unstable transition toward a yet undefined order—several trajectories for the BRICS can be envisioned. A scenario of consolidation would see the group strengthening its internal coordination, institutionalizing cooperation across finance, infrastructure, and diplomacy, and emerging as a coherent governance bloc capable of advancing inclusive reforms within multilateral institutions. Conversely, a scenario of fragmentation would result from diverging national interests, economic asymmetries, and geopolitical rivalries, reducing the BRICS to a loose and episodic coalition, ineffective in promoting systemic change. A third possibility, the pragmatic coalition scenario, envisions flexible, issue-based cooperation—on trade, climate finance, and/or development—without a single center of leadership, enabling selective progress on specific global issues but limiting the group's capacity to drive comprehensive institutional reform. The trajectory the BRICS will ultimately follow will depend on their ability to clarify internal governance mechanisms, enhance transparency and accountability in new institutions, and prioritize inclusive development outcomes over narrow geopolitical influence. For Western powers, acknowledging the BRICS as a structural feature of the evolving global order—rather than as a temporary anomaly—requires renewed diplomatic engagement, accelerated reform of legacy institutions, and a genuine commitment to multilateralism. For the Global South, agency can be strengthened by building cross-regional coalitions, leveraging competition between major powers, and promoting institutional reforms that safeguard procedural equity, regional representation, and accountability.

Ultimately, the capacity of the international community to address shared global challenges—climate change, technological transitions, growing inequality—will hinge on whether the emerging order evolves toward plural cooperation or renewed antagonism. The BRICS signal that a structural transformation is underway; yet the form it will take—consolidation, fragmentation, or pragmatic coalition—remains uncertain. The most desirable outcome would be a plural and cooperative system characterized by multiple centers of power embedded in robust, inclusive institutions that give voice to all. Failing to construct such an order risks deepening divisions and delaying the collective responses urgently required to confront threats that affect humanity as a whole.

Index[1]

[1] Note: Page numbers followed by 'n' refer to notes.

F. Petrone, *The BRICS and the Transformation of Global Power*, https://doi.org/10.1007/978-3-032-23540-4

The manufacturer's authorised representative in the EU is Springer
Nature Customer Service Centre GmbH, Europaplatz 3, 69115 Heidelberg,
Germany. If you have any concerns regarding our products, please
contact ProductSafety@springernature.com

Printed and bound by CPI Group (UK) Ltd, Croydon, CR0 4YY
16/09/2026
02217786-0002